Goutham M. Menon, PhD
Editor

Using the Internet as a Research Tool for Social Work and Human Services

Using the Internet as a Research Tool for Social Work and Human Services has been co-published as *Journal of Technology in Human Services*, Volume 19, Numbers 2/3 2002.

Pre-publication REVIEWS, COMMENTARIES, EVALUATIONS . . .

"Summarizes the strengths and weaknesses of Internet-based research. . . . Provides an innovative look at improving survey samples and offers suggestions for overcoming sampling bias. The chapter by Murray and Fisher on the potential limitless ability of the Internet to assist research, juxtaposed with Gonzalez's call for careful scrutiny of Internet research will help social science researchers make informed decisions."

Sherry Edwards, PhD, MSW
Assistant Professor of Sociology Social Work, and Criminal Justice The University of South Carolina, Pembroke

The Haworth Press, Inc.

Using the Internet as a Research Tool for Social Work and Human Services

Using the Internet as a Research Tool for Social Work and Human Services has been co-published simultaneously as *Journal of Technology in Human Services*, Volume 19, Numbers 2/3 2002.

The *Journal of Technology in Human Services* Monographic "Separates" (formerly the *Computers in Human Services* Series)*

Below is a list of " separates," which in serials librarianship means a special issue simultaneously published as a special journal issue or double-issue *and* as a "separate" hardbound monograph. (This is a format which we also call a "DocuSerial.")

"Separates" are published because specialized libraries or professionals may wish to purchase a specific thematic issue by itself in a format which can be separately cataloged and shelved, as opposed to purchasing the journal on an on-going basis. Faculty members may also more easily consider a "separate" for classroom adoption.

"Separates" are carefully classified separately with the major book jobbers so that the journal tie-in can be noted on new book order slips to avoid duplicate purchasing.

You may wish to visit Haworth's Website at . . .

http://www.HaworthPress.com

. . . to search our online catalog for complete tables of contents of these separates and related publications.

You may also call 1-800-HAWORTH (outside US/Canada: 607-722-5857), or Fax 1-800-895-0582 (outside US/Canada: 607-771-0012), or e-mail at:

getinfo@haworthpressinc.com

Using the Internet as a Research Tool for Social Work and Human Services, edited by Goutham M. Menon, PhD (Vol.19, No. 2/3, 2002). *Explores ways to use the Internet in many aspects of social work research, including the development of online studies and psychological testing.*

New Advances in Technology for Social Work Education and Practice, edited by Julie Miller-Cribbs, PhD (Vol. 18, No. 3/4, 2001). *"A valuable tool for educators who want to introduce students of social work to the numerous applications of technology within the field. . . . Goes a long way toward helping social work become proactive in its approach to technology integration within the field." (Sharon D. Johnson, PhD, Assistant Professor, Department of Social Work, University of Missouri, St. Louis)*

Using Technology in Human Services Education: Going the Distance, edited by Goutham M. Menon, PhD, and Nancy K. Brown, PhD (Vol 18, No. 1/2, 2001). *"A REFRESHINGLY REALISTIC AND BALANCED COLLECTION . . . . Highlights many innovative efforts in both education and practice. Will be extremely valuable in courses on technology in social work, or for courses examining emerging trends in social work practice." (Paul P. Freddolino, PhD, Professor and Coordinator of Distance Education, School of Social Work, Michigan State University, East Lansing)*

Human Services Online: A New Arena for Service Delivery, edited by Jerry Finn, PhD, and Gary Holden, DSW (Vol. 17, No. 1/2/3, 2000). *Focuses on the ways that human services are using the Internet for service delivery, social change, and resource development as more and more agencies can be found on the Internet.*

Computers and Information Technology in Social Work: Education, Training, and Practice, edited by Jo Ann R. Coe, PhD, and Goutham M. Menon, PhD (Vol. 16, No. 2/3, 1999). *Discusses the impact that recent technological advances have had on social work practice and education. Social workers and educators will discover ideas and projects that were presented at a week-long conference presented at the University of South Carolina College of Social Work. This unique book covers a wide range of topics, such as different aspects of technology applied to assist those in helping professions, how computers can be used in child protective cases in order to practice more effectively, social services via videoconferencing, and much more.*

Information Technologies: Teaching to Use–Using to Teach, edited by Frank B. Raymond III, DSW, Leon Ginsberg, PhD, and Debra Gohagan, MSW, ACSW, LISW* (Vol. 15, No. 2/3, 1998). *Explores examples of the use of technology to teach social work knowledge, values, and skills across the curriculum.*

The History and Function of the Target Cities Management Information Systems, edited by Matthew G. Hile, PhD* (Vol. 14, No. 3/4, 1998). *"Essential reading for anyone invested in improving the coordination and delivery of substance abuse services in large metropolitan areas." (Albert D. Farrell, PhD, Professor of Psychology, Virginia Commonwealth University, Richmond)*

Human Services in the Information Age, edited by Jackie Rafferty, MS, Jan Steyaert, and David Colombi* (Vol. 12, No. 1/2/3/4, 1996). *"Anyone interested in the current state of the development of human service information systems of all types needs to read this book." (Walter F. LaMendola, PhD, Consultant, Wheat Ridge, CO)*

Electronic Tools for Social Work Practice and Education, edited by Hy Resnick, PhD* (Vol. 11, No. 1/2/3/4, 1994). *"Opens a new world of opportunities for readers by introducing a variety of electronic tools available when working with various clients." (Ram A. Cnaan, PhD, Associate Professor, School of Social Work, University of Pennsylvania)*

Technology in People Services: Research, Theory, and Applications, edited by Marcos Leiderman, MSW, Charles Guzzetta, EdD, Leny Struminger, PhD, and Menachem Monnickendam, PhD, MSW* (Vol. 9, No. 1/2/3/4, 1993). *"Honest reporting and inquiry into the opportunities and limitations for administrators, managers, supervisors, clinicians, service providers, consumers, and clients . . . A well-integrated and in-depth examination." (John P. Flynn, PhD, Associate Director for Instructional Computing, University Computing Services and Professor of Social Work, Western Michigan University)*

Computer Applications in Mental Health: Education and Evaluation, edited by Marvin J. Miller, MD* (Vol. 8, No. 3/4, 1992). *"Describes computer programs designed specifically for mental health clinicians and their work in both private practice and institutional treatment settings." (SciTech Book News)*

Computers for Social Change and Community Organizing, edited by John Downing, PhD, Robert Fasano, MSW, Patricia Friedland, MLS, Michael McCullough, AM, Terry Mizrahi, PhD, and Jeremy Shapiro, PhD* (Vol. 8, No. 1, 1991). *This landmark volume presents an original and–until now–unavailable perspective on the uses of computers for community- and social-change-based organizations.*

Computer Literacy in Human Services Education, edited by Richard L. Reinoehl and B. Jeanne Mueller* (Vol. 7, No. 1/2/3/4, 1990). *This volume provides a unique and notable contribution to the investigation and exemplification of computer literacy in human services education.*

Computer Literacy in Human Services, edited by Richard L. Reinoehl and Thomas Hanna* (Vol. 6, No. 1/2/3/4, 1990). *"Includes a diversity of articles on many of the most important practical and conceptual issues associated with the use of computer technology in the human services." (Adult Residential Care)*

The Impact of Information Technology on Social Work Practice, edited by Ram A. Cnaan, PhD, and Phyllida Parsloe, PhD* (Vol. 5, No. 1/2, 1989). *International experts confront the urgent need for social work practice to move into the computer age.*

A Casebook of Computer Applications in the Social and Human Services, edited by Walter LaMendola, PhD, Bryan Glastonbury, and Stuart Toole* (Vol. 4, No. 1/2/3/4, 1989). *"Makes for engaging and enlightening reading in the rapidly expanding field of information technology in the human services." (Wallace Gingerich, PhD, Associate Professor, School of Social Welfare, University of Wisconsin-Milwaukee)*

Technology and Human Service Delivery: Challenges and a Critical Perspective, edited by John W. Murphy, PhD, and John T. Pardeck, PhD, MSW* (Vol. 3, No. 1/2, 1988). *"A much-needed, critical examination of whether and how computers can improve social services . . . Essential reading for social workers in the field and for scholars interested in how computers alter social systems." (Charles Ess, PhD, Assistant Professor of Philosophy, Morningside College)*

Research in Mental Health Computing: The Next Five Years, edited by John H. Greist, MD, Judith A. Carroll, PhD, Harold P. Erdman, PhD, Marjorie H. Klein, PhD, and Cecil R. Wurster, MA* (Vol. 2, No. 3/4, 1988). *"Provides a clear and lucid perspective on the state of research in mental health computing." (David Servan-Schreiber, MD, Western Psychiatric Institute & Clinic and Department of Computer Science, Carnegie Mellon University)*

Using the Internet as a Research Tool for Social Work and Human Services has been co-published simultaneously as *Journal of Technology in Human Services*™, Volume 19, Numbers 2/3 2002.

The development, preparation, and publication of this work has been undertaken with great care. However, the publisher, employees, editors, and agents of The Haworth Press and all imprints of The Haworth Press, Inc., including The Haworth Medical Press® and Pharmaceutical Products Press®, are not responsible for any errors contained herein or for consequences that may ensue from use of materials or information contained in this work. Opinions expressed by the author(s) are not necessarily those of The Haworth Press, Inc. With regard to case studies, identities and circumstances of individuals discussed herein have been changed to protect confidentiality. Any resemblance to actual persons, living or dead, is entirely coincidental.

Cover design by Thomas J. Mayshock Jr.

Library of Congress Cataloging-in-Publication Data

Using the Internet as a Research Tool for Social Work and Human Services / Goutham M. Menon, editor.
    p. cm.
    "Co-published simultaneously as Journal of Technology in Human Services volume 19, numbers 2/3 2002."
    Includes bibliographical references and index.
    ISBN 0-7890-1447-5 (hard : alk. paper) – ISBN 0-7890-1448-3 (pbk : alk. paper)
    1. Social service–Research–Computer network resources. 2. Human services–Research–Computer network resources. 3. Internet. I. Menon, Goutham M. II. Journal of technology in human services. v. 19, no 2/3 2002 (Supplement)
  HV29 .8 .U85 2002
  361'.07'2–dc21   2002002580

Using the Internet as a Research Tool for Social Work and Human Services

Goutham M. Menon, PhD
Editor

Using the Internet as a Research Tool for Social Work and Human Services has been co-published simultaneously as *Journal of Technology in Human Services*, Volume 19, Numbers 2/3 2002.

The Haworth Press, Inc.
New York • London • Oxford

Indexing, Abstracting & Website/Internet Coverage

This section provides you with a list of major indexing & abstracting services. That is to say, each service began covering this periodical during the year noted in the right column. Most Websites which are listed below have indicated that they will either post, disseminate, compile, archive, cite or alert their own Website users with research-based content from this work. (This list is as current as the copyright date of this publication.)

(continued)

(continued)

Special Bibliographic Notes related to special journal issues (separates) and indexing/abstracting:

- indexing/abstracting services in this list will also cover material in any "separate" that is co-published simultaneously with Haworth's special thematic journal issue or DocuSerial. Indexing/abstracting usually covers material at the article/chapter level.
- monographic co-editions are intended for either non-subscribers or libraries which intend to purchase a second copy for their circulating collections.
- monographic co-editions are reported to all jobbers/wholesalers/approval plans. The source journal is listed as the "series" to assist the prevention of duplicate purchasing in the same manner utilized for books-in-series.
- to facilitate user/access services all indexing/abstracting services are encouraged to utilize the co-indexing entry note indicated at the bottom of the first page of each article/chapter/contribution.
- this is intended to assist a library user of any reference tool (whether print, electronic, online, or CD-ROM) to locate the monographic version if the library has purchased this version but not a subscription to the source journal.
- individual articles/chapters in any Haworth publication are also available through the Haworth Document Delivery Service (HDDS).

Using the Internet as a Research Tool for Social Work and Human Services

CONTENTS

ABOUT THE EDITOR

Goutham M. Menon, PhD, is Assistant Professor at the College of Social Work, University of South Carolina, Columbia. He is a co-author of the books *Using Technology in Human Services Education: Going the Distance* and *Computers and Information Technology in Social Work: Education, Training and Practice.* His area of expertise lies in the utilization of technology for education and practice, especially in the area of electronic advocacy and Internet-based research. Dr. Menon serves on the editorial board of the *Journal of Technology in Human Services.*

Using the Internet as a Tool for Research

Goutham M. Menon

The words "Internet research" often conjure up the image of a person sitting in front of a computer monitor typing keywords in online search engines. Most writings on "Internet research" dwell on how fascinating and easy it is to get information using the World Wide Web. While surfing the Internet for information is a legitimate "research" experience, its use only for that will be a major travesty to a medium of communication that has exponentially captured the attention of millions of users and which has the capability to shape and mold minds in the years to come.

The Internet is especially intriguing for its lack of geographical boundaries. A virtual community in networks of nodes and fiber optic cables may seem to be elusive to capture useful data. But with the growing popularity of online discussion groups, chat rooms, and other communication entities, this world is rich with information that will be of interest to social scientists around the world.

Researchers have been working in this area for these few long years. And the credibility of this type of research was best exemplified by the creation of the Association of Internet Researchers (www.aoir.org), an organization devoted to the scholarly study of the Internet. Interest in this area has been growing and researchers around the world have begun to experiment with the many nuances this medium has to offer. Ranging from simple online surveys to more sophisticated ethnographic studies of virtual communities, researchers have found the Internet to be an area

Goutham M. Menon, PhD, is Assistant Professor at the College of Social Work, University of South Carolina, Columbia, SC 29208 (E-mail: goutham.menon@ sc.edu).

[Haworth co-indexing entry note]: "Using the Internet as a Tool for Research." Menon, Goutham M. Co-published simultaneously in *Journal of Technology in Human Services* (The Haworth Press, Inc.) Vol. 19, No. 2/3, 2002, pp. 1-3; and: *Using the Internet as a Research Tool for Social Work and Human Services* (ed: Goutham M. Menon) The Haworth Press, Inc., 2002, pp. 1-3. Single or multiple copies of this article are available for a fee from The Haworth Document Delivery Service [1-800-HAWORTH, 9:00 a.m. - 5:00 p.m. (EST). E-mail address: getinfo@haworthpressinc.com].

of much sociological and psychological importance. This volume tries to give an overarching view of what is possible in this field and what steps researchers must take to have a fruitful research protocol online. The contributors for this book come from myriad fields and their work best exemplifies the field of Internet research today.

Danielle Murray and Jeffrey Fisher provide us with a comprehensive look at the use of Internet methodologies. They explicate the processes of online data collection, and discuss issues regarding sampling and representativeness of the subjects selected. They conclude by highlighting the various areas of research that could benefit from the use of Internet-based methods and throw light on the practical limitations that researchers might face. J. E. Gonzalez's paper further dwells on the issue of sampling and describes methodological errors that may occur with present-day use of the Internet for research purposes. He makes a case for researchers to use thoughtful protocols to limit errors as much as possible.

Epstein and Klinkenberg discuss the process of developing and deploying an Internet-based study that sought to replicate the results of a traditionally administered questionnaire. Replicating a study dealing with HIV risk behaviors, they used an online survey to target a gay and lesbian sample. Sharon Kleinman's article highlights the fact that there are "people behind the computer screens" and that the study of computer-mediated groups must be handled cautiously. She describes the study of a listserv group that deals with issues of interest to women in science and engineering. It looked at how some of the women in these fields are using computer-mediated groups as resources for social support, information, role models, and mentors.

Psychological testing has found a new avenue in the area of the World Wide Web. Azy Barak and Nicole English provide for us some of the prospects and limitations of psychological testing on the Internet in their thought-provoking article. Using the Internet for training is also catching on in many areas in health and human services. Philip Ouellette and Richard Briscoe highlight a technology-supported training environment to enhance the development of research skills of undergraduate level multicultural mental health researchers.

Georgia Quartaro and Terry Spier explore some issues related to an Internet-based study dealing with lesbian clients' perception of their lesbian feminist therapists. They used a web-based survey to conduct their research. Cyber culture and the study of virtual communities is a fascinating field. Susan Kinnevy and Guy Enosh recount the problems they faced in the study of a virtual community and talk about the daily interactions of peace activists in a virtual community devoted to non-violent solutions to world problems. Finally, Paul Montgomery and David Ritchie provide a look at automating a research study on the Internet. They describe a simple program for administering an experiment dependent on measuring response time over the Web.

As you can see, this compilation of work done in the area of Internet research provides some compelling conceptual pieces supplemented with actual research done using this medium. I hope you will find this volume meaningful in your Internet research endeavors.

The Internet:
A Virtually Untapped Tool for Research

Danielle M. Murray
Jeffrey D. Fisher

SUMMARY. Internet methodologies are often overlooked in research. This review presents evidence that using the Internet to recruit participants and collect data is not only feasible, but may also be less expensive and time-consuming than traditional data collection methods. Additionally, Internet data collection can yield a more representative participant sample than more traditional data collection methods, while retaining equivalent, if not better, psychometric properties. Different areas of research that could benefit from the use of the Internet-based methods are explored. Overall benefits of Internet-based data collection, and practical limitations and how to overcome them, are discussed. *[Article copies available for a fee from The Haworth Document Delivery Service: 1-800-HAWORTH. E-mail address: <getinfo@haworthpressinc.com> Website: <http://www.HaworthPress.com> © 2002 by The Haworth Press, Inc. All rights reserved.]*

Danielle M. Murray, MA, and Jeffrey D. Fisher, PhD, are affiliated with the Department of Psychology, University of Connecticut.

This work was supported by Grant 1RO1MH59473 from the National Institutes of Mental Health, awarded to Jeffrey D. Fisher, PhD.

Address correspondence to: Danielle M. Murray, Department of Psychology, U-Box 20, 406 Babbidge Road, University of Connecticut, Storrs, CT 06269-1020 (dmurray@psych.psy.uconn.edu).

[Haworth co-indexing entry note]: "The Internet: A Virtually Untapped Tool for Research." Murray, Danielle M., and Jeffrey D. Fisher. Co-published simultaneously in *Journal of Technology in Human Services* (The Haworth Press, Inc.) Vol. 19, No. 2/3, 2002, pp. 5-18; and: *Using the Internet as a Research Tool for Social Work and Human Services* (ed: Goutham M. Menon) The Haworth Press, Inc., 2002, pp. 5-18. Single or multiple copies of this article are available for a fee from The Haworth Document Delivery Service [1-800-HAWORTH, 9:00 a.m. - 5:00 p.m. (EST). E-mail address: getinfo@haworthpressinc.com].

KEYWORDS. Internet, research, World Wide Web, methods, computer, psychology

Social sciences research has traditionally been conducted using university undergraduate students as participants (Buchanan & Smith, 1999). This population is an easy-to-access, convenient, and inexpensive group of potential participants for all types of social science research (Birnbaum, 1999; Roberts, Scott, & Baluch, 1993). University students tend to be European-American, of higher socioeconomic status, are more educated than the general United States population, and their age range is restricted, with an average of less than 30 years (Smith & Leigh, 1997). Furthermore, studies conducted with university students as participants often suffer from having far more women than men in their sample, as most students enrolled in social science courses are female (Smith & Leigh, 1997). This is *not* representative of the broader population to which we try to generalize our findings (Bourke, 1999; Lennon, Burns, & Rowold, 1995; Roberts et al., 1993). Nevertheless, most studies fail to limit the generalizability of their findings to the actual population accessed, and may not only assume generalizability to the entire U. S. population, but may assume broader applicability of research results as well. Another consideration is that a population of university psychology students does not represent many of the groups important to the study of critical problems, such as those with particular behavior patterns and illnesses, people with certain stigmatized conditions, or those who would otherwise not be enrolled in a university.

In recent years, the Internet and the World Wide Web (WWW) have gained international popularity due to the increased access and decreased cost of the necessary technology and software. It is estimated that between 30 and 97 million people world wide currently use the Internet (Buchanan & Smith, 1999; GVU's 7th WWW User Survey, 1997; Lakeman, 1997), and there seems to be no decrease in the number of people who "get connected" every day. Estimates indicate that the number of Internet users grows at a rate of 10% every month, virtually doubling every few months (Mehta & Sivadas, 1995). In a web-based user survey which reached participants from all of the U. S. states, Asia, Canada, Australia, New Zealand, Africa, Europe, Central and South America, Antarctica, the West Indies and the Middle East (GVU's 10th WWW User Survey, 1998), it was shown that over 30% of the respondents used their WWW browser more than nine times a day, nearly 40% had been using the Internet for four to six years, and an additional 15%

had been using it for more than seven years. Furthermore, the vast majority of respondents (80%) said they felt very comfortable using the Internet. Ages ranged from 10 to over 85 years old, approximately 35% of respondents were female, 87% were Caucasian and the remaining 13% were Asian, African-American, Hispanic, Latino, Indigenous or multi-racial, demonstrating the diversity of the population that can be accessed through the Internet (Hewson, Laurent, & Vogel, 1996; Kelly & Oldham, 1997). While these statistics show that the samples accessed are still predominantly Caucasian, they demonstrate great diversity with respect to age, and include more males than traditional participant pools and a promising international population. Overall, use of the Internet for data collection has already shown an increase in diversity over that of college student populations, and as computers become more accessible to the general public, the diversity of potential samples will increase dramatically.

In 1994, the first publicly accessible Web-based user survey was launched and since then there have been hundreds of such surveys in many different domains, including psychology and the medical, nursing, counseling, market research, and information technology fields (Birnbaum, 1999; Childress & Asamen, 1998; GVU, 1999; Klemm & Nolan, 1998; Suchard, Hadfield, Elliot, & Kennedy, 1998), among others. For administering surveys widely, tens of thousands of newsgroups (a domain on the Internet devoted to the discussion of a specified topic) and listservs (automated mailing lists) worldwide make access to hard-to-find and specialty populations easy (Stone, 1998). Virtually any population one could imagine has some sort of Internet user group or listserv which can be used by researchers to access the relevant population for survey research, observation, contact or recruitment.

Despite the presence of a rapidly growing resource like the WWW, researchers have been reticent to accept the new technologies, and have been even slower in incorporating the many uses of the WWW into their methodological repertoire (Mehta & Sivadas, 1995; Subramanian, McAfee, & Getzinger, 1997). For the present manuscript, we conducted an extensive review on the use of the Internet for participant recruitment and data collection.[1] Special emphases were placed on the comparison of the psychometric properties of paper and pencil versus computerized and Internet formats, and on the comparison of sample representativeness associated with "in-person" and "online" formats. It was hypothesized that while university participant pools are the most widely used participant sample, Internet-administered formats would yield a more diverse and representative sample of the U. S. population than traditional university student "in-person" samples involving paper and pencil techniques, while still retaining comparable, if not better, psychometric properties than paper and pencil versions.

IN-PERSON VERSUS INTERNET DATA COLLECTION METHODS

Despite initial reluctance to consider computer-administered research a viable option, psychology and education researchers have been using computers for data collection in the laboratories for decades (Lautenschlager & Flaherty, 1990). In the early 1990s, "disk by mail" (DBM) surveys, in which researchers mail out a copy of their survey on a floppy disk for the participant to access at their leisure in the privacy of their own home, were introduced (Dahl, 1992). The benefit of DBM over traditional paper and pencil surveys mailed to the home was that with DBM, researchers did not have to enter the data into the computer, thereby eliminating many hours of labor and human error. Electronic mail (E-Mail) based surveys were quick to follow DBM, and provide the added benefit of being able to access a larger population for less cost and time, as well as more cost-efficient "reminders." Computers have been widely used in research laboratories, and using the Internet to collect data is merely an extension of this oft-used computer technology. While some researchers have voiced concerns about the interchangeability of computerized versus paper and pencil research methods (Dahl, 1992; Webster & Compeau, 1996; Whitener & Klein, 1995), some studies claim that computer-administered methods reduce social desirability responding (SDR) by creating a greater sense of anonymity for participants (Childress & Asamen, 1998; Dahl, 1992; Hewson et al., 1996; Webster & Compeau, 1996; Whitener & Klein, 1995). Computerized methods have also been shown to reduce, if not completely eliminate, the effects of experimenter bias by having the impartial and unbiased computer act and be perceived by the participant as the experimenter (Hewson et al., 1996; Mehta & Sivadas, 1995).

Several studies have directly compared functionally equivalent paper and pencil and Internet formats of questionnaires (Buchanan & Smith, 1999; Murray & Fisher, 1999; Smith & Leigh, 1997). Smith and Leigh (1997) did so with a group of university psychology students and a separate group of Internet users, all of whom filled out a human sexuality questionnaire. With respect to demographics, while 95% of the student sample was under the age of 30 and 80% were female, only 65% of the

Internet sample were under the age of 30, and only 26% were female. Aside from age and gender differences, the two samples had comparable ethnic, religious, sexual orientation and marital status representation. Buchanan and Smith (1999) found parallel demographic patterns to Smith and Leigh (1997) for the university student vs. Internet samples with a common self-monitoring personality test, though the Internet sample yielded an equivalent female-to-male ratio. Murray and Fisher (1999) likewise yielded parallel demographic patterns, and demonstrated an *oversampling* of females for the target population (motorcyclists). Further, there were no appreciable differences in the survey results between the paper and pencil and the Internet versions in these three studies.

Emerging research (Buchanan & Smith, 1999; Murray & Fisher, 1999; Michalak & Szabo, 1998) has shown that Internet methods have similar and sometimes better psychometric properties (e.g., factor loadings, reliabilities, and goodness-of-fit indices) than traditional paper and pencil data collection methods. It was proposed that the greater heterogeneity of the Internet-based sample provided a "clearer picture . . . of the test's factor structure" (Buchanan & Smith, 1999, p. 139). Overall, there is suggestive evidence that while results may not differ between Internet and in-person administrations, Internet samples may provide a more representative sample of the U. S. population than university students. While one must be careful to note that Internet data collection restricts potential participants to the group of people who have Internet access, that group is much larger than the very small number of people who are enrolled in undergraduate classes at U. S. universities. Also, it is evident that the Internet attracts a much more varied sample of people than that which can be represented in a university participant pool population.

ADVANTAGES OF INTERNET RESEARCH

Sample characteristics. There are many ways in which the Internet provides critical benefits over in-person data collection methods, such as with respect to sample size recruited per unit time and accessibility to specialized populations. Some studies have resulted in Internet samples up to four times larger than in-person samples (Buchanan & Smith, 1999; Murray & Fisher, 1999), and suggest that data collection via the Internet per unit time is much more efficient and cost-effective than mailed or in-person surveys (Mehta & Sivadas, 1995). Additionally, studies collecting data via the Internet have reported response rates of approximately 60%, equal to those of mail and phone surveys (Sell, 1997). The Internet is also a rich resource for those in search of specialized, stigmatized, or otherwise hard-to-reach populations (Hewson et al., 1996; Subramanian et al., 1997) which would be impossible to recruit in an undergraduate student population. Recruiting such samples with methods other than the Internet would be extremely time intensive and expensive, often to the point of being unfeasible. For example, if one wishes to survey people with STDs, certain psychological disorders, speech impediments, cancer survivors, or even a population of transsexuals, a quick search online results in several bulletin boards, listservs, and chat rooms from which active recruitment of participants is relatively easy. Other specific or hard-to-reach populations, for example, motorcyclists, skydivers, musicians, and the like, can also be accessed easily via the Internet.

Clearly a researcher would find far more participants from a stigmatized or specialized group through an anonymous posting on topic-relevant bulletin boards and chat rooms than by posting flyers at a university or within the typical community, or by putting up a participant sign-up sheet for undergraduate participants (Michalak & Szabo, 1998). To locate and administer research protocols to these types of populations outside of the Internet could pose a serious financial and time burden on a researcher, especially one who is not funded by a large grant. The Internet clearly provides much greater access to a wider geographic range of participants for unfunded undergraduate and graduate students, unfunded professors, and those conducting research from abroad, especially those in third world countries. In cases where data *collection* cannot be conducted via the Internet, participant *recruitment* can, which could ultimately increase study sample sizes and representativeness (Biesecker & DeRenzo, 1995). Many research interests in the social sciences involve sensitive topics, such as disease and addiction, and online recruiting can enhance the sense of confidentiality, on the part of the participants, associated with contacting the researcher and signing up for the study.

Cost and time benefits. Many studies highlight the cost- and time-efficiency of data collection via the Internet compared to that of phone, mail, or in-person surveys (Fawcett & Buhle, 1995; Lakeman, 1997; Murray & Fisher, 1999; Suchard et al., 1998). Since the data is being collected electronically, it is possible to create a program that not only collects it but also converts and sends it to a statistical package of choice (Birnbaum, 1999; Subramanian et al., 1997; for a discussion of technological aspects of web-based research, see Kieley, 1996). This more automated arrangement increases the quality of the data because there is less potential for human error, vastly reduces personnel costs associated with questionnaire administration and data entry, and speeds up the data analytic process significantly (Subramanian et al., 1997). In contrast to in-person surveys, Murray and Fisher (1999) found that Internet data collection saved approximately 210 hours of data collection and entry time, as well as 24 reams of paper! Presentation of materials on the Internet also obviates duplicating costs, and cost and time spent collating materials; also the inconvenience and cost associated with space for archiving and storing data (Kelly & Oldham, 1997). To the contentment of environmentalists, using the computer to collect data saves trees, as well as the need for recycling (Mehta & Sivadas, 1995; Murray & Fisher, 1999; Subramanian et al., 1997). Even when considering the expenses associated with setting up the computer programs, most researchers will find Internet data collection to be more cost-efficient.

Another benefit of Internet data collection is that one can write the program not to accept incomplete data forms, which could cut down, or completely eliminate problems associated with missing values. Further, programs can be written with a "skip" function such that specific responses to certain questions (e.g., do you use injection drugs) can allow the participant to skip subsequent questions (e.g., about injection drug use) that may be irrelevant. This can significantly reduce response burden on the participant, and foster higher quality responses to the remaining items. The use of the Internet also makes it easier for researchers to make minor modifications or clarifications to the experimental materials if deemed necessary, since it affords the luxury of viewing the data immediately (Mehta & Sivadas, 1995). Minor modifications to materials take a matter of seconds or minutes to complete, and there are no associated paper and copying costs.

Motivation and remuneration. Some researchers argue that the motivation of people who complete online surveys may differ from that of more traditional participants (Buchanan & Smith, 1997). Given that online participants generally seek out studies in which to participate, they are likely to be *more* interested in the topic of study, and therefore more motivated to participate and also to respond more thoughtfully than traditional participants. One reason for this is that the topic of focus may be personally relevant to them (e.g., they are HIV positive, they are overweight), which makes the findings of the studies on these more "specialized" topics more ecologically valid and generalizable. Further, since it has also been shown that Internet samples for more general surveys (e.g., attitudes towards sexuality) are more representative than college student samples, research with these populations *also* yields greater ecological validity and generalizeability. It can also be argued that participants may be more motivated to complete an online survey because they can do it on their own time, in the privacy and convenience of their home, and are not subjected to the experimenter's schedule (Hewson et al., 1996).

Another relevant issue is that of offering financial remuneration to online participants. While some researchers have stated that this is not possible (Mehta & Sivadas, 1995), others have found it to be quite feasible (D. M. Murray & Fisher, 1999). A recent online survey successfully offered $5 to participants in return for their participation. Less than one-fourth of the 692 participants asked for the $5 remuneration, in contrast to the more than 95% of participants who completed the same survey in person (D. M. Murray & Fisher, 1999). One reason for this may have been due to the fact that participants are more personally involved in the topic at focus, are able to complete online materials at their leisure and felt less "coerced" than those who filled out the survey in person.

Possible lines of research. Understandably, the most common use for Internet data collection technology has been correlational questionnaire and survey research (Childress & Asamen, 1998; Hewson et al., 1996). However, the use of the Internet should not be restricted to these research paradigms. Many studies, including experimental research, currently being conducted in laboratories with the participant sitting at a desk with paper and pencil, or even at a computer terminal (Smith & Leigh, 1997), could be done via the Internet.

Studies in personality, psycholinguistics, experimental, cognitive, and developmental psychology, discourse analysis, social and industrial/organizational psychological research, testing any number of paradigms such as prejudice, word recognition, perceptual learning and visual perception, decision-making, peer behavioral nominations, attitudes, or worker motivation, among others, can easily be conducted over the Internet. With the addition of some still costly audio and video software and hardware, such as CuseeME, RealAudio and RealVideo (for a more in-depth discussion of video conferencing equipment and specifications, see http://aloha.acs.ohio-state.edu/videoc.html), real-time interactive or simulation studies, person-perception, impression formation, and even intervention studies could be conducted via the Internet (Childress & Asamen, 1998; Subramanian et al., 1997). Computer programs which randomly assign online participants to conditions in factorial designs are already in existence (Birnbaum, 1999), enabling researchers to conduct experimental studies, equivalent and virtually identical to those conducted in the lab, from remote locations.

Human sexuality and personality researchers have already benefited from the use of the Internet, as the anonymous nature and convenience of not having to travel to participate have facilitated a more comfortable environment for participants in studies of highly sensitive subject matters (Binik, Mah, & Kiesler, 1999; Hewson et al., 1996). Researchers have likewise used the WWW for short-term longitudinal projects, wherein a participant logs onto the site multiple times at specified intervals to measure recall and memory decay (Morrow & McKee, 1998). With careful planning and diligent follow-ups, longer-term longitudinal research can be made accessible and feasible to researchers by increasing access to participants over time, and improving the ease with which reminders and materials can be dispensed, namely through e-mail. Perhaps due to the cost-efficiency of Internet recruitment, data collection, and participant retention, long-term follow-up can be administered and maintained more easily, conveniently, and frequently than at present. In fact, opportunities for follow-up studies may exist via the Internet in contexts never even contemplated in the past.

Elicitation research (e.g., live focus groups, preliminary open-ended questionnaires), often done to assist in designing the preliminary phases of interventions or research materials such as questionnaires, can easily be conducted on the Internet with the help of real-time chat groups, also known as Internet relay chat rooms (I.R.C.). This technology can help to facilitate focus groups in general, and more representative ones in particular, as the participants could remain anonymous and in the comfort of their own homes, and would not be forced to travel to partake in the discussion. Also, a host of naturalistic observations can be made by unobtrusively monitoring online sites (e.g., erotic material sites, hate group sites) and communications. While the ethics of taking direct quotes from online postings without informed consent has not yet been clarified or codified, researchers can unobtrusively monitor and report on a whole host of behaviors, such as online communication patterns, prejudice, disclosure, or depression, through online chat rooms, bulletin boards, and newsgroups, provided that no identifying information is presented in the manuscript (King, 1996).

Many language studies can be conducted via the Internet (Hewson et al., 1996). In psycholinguistics, for example, word recognition and word categorization studies could quite easily be posted to the WWW. Additionally, researchers interested in performing cross-cultural research and in accessing foreign participants can post online materials in any number of languages in an effort to target participants from other nations and cultures, without having to be physically present in that country. More broadly, the potential to post questionnaires in foreign languages via the Internet has tremendous implications for cross-cultural research in virtually every area of research (Subramanian et al., 1997).

LIMITATIONS AND HOW TO OVERCOME THEM

While Internet-based research has many advantages, it also has several limitations that need to be addressed. Perhaps the most obvious is that *not everyone has access to a computer*, let alone the Internet (Mehta & Sivadas, 1995). While this is a problem if one is striving for a truly representative sample, in most circumstances the sample accessed through the Internet would be the most representative that the researcher would be able to obtain without huge data collection costs, and would certainly be more representative than the standard–undergraduate students. Moreover, more and more people around the world are gaining Internet access at home, in the office, and in schools. Many public and school libraries now have Internet-accessible computers available to students and faculty, which facilitates accessibility to lower-income populations (GVU, 1999).

A second limitation to Internet research is *the availability of the technology to the researcher*. Depending on the desires of the researcher, a project will have varying levels of technological needs. Some projects, such as a simple questionnaire, may only require a reliable server in which to collect and store data, while others, such as person perception studies, may require the use of computer video equipment and a server that can run at sufficiently high speeds to transmit video feed. For most researchers and universities, this should not be a problem. However, researchers who do not have access to sufficient computer and support systems (i.e., do not have a reliable server, do not have computers with sufficient memory or speed) may not find certain types of Internet research feasible. If a server is prone to crashing or server maintenance is expected to occur frequently, data collection would be interrupted, which could in turn adversely affect study results. As the technology becomes more reliable and less expensive, this problem will become less and less of a concern.

Bogus data or multiple responders. A third limitation is that it can be difficult to control for bogus data or multiple responses from a single participant (Buchanan & Smith, 1999). Two reasonable solutions to controlling for multiple responses from one person is to record the IP address of each participant and to assign individual passwords to each participant. While IP addresses are not a completely stable indicator of who is responding to an online study, in conjunction with time stamps and the patterns in the data itself, they serve a general function of monitoring responses. The researcher can decide for her- or himself what action should be taken in the case that there are multiple responses from the same computer. In some cases, it could be that two or more different people have used the same computer, or it could be that one individual is submitting multiple responses. Taking a good look at the response patterns from entries from the same IP address may provide insight as to whether both responses came from the same individual or not.

While assigning individual passwords to participants extends the data collection process a bit, it provides heightened security. Individuals wishing to participate in the study would be given a password with which they can access the online survey. Only those possessing passwords can access the survey, and each password would only be valid once, thereby reducing the threat of multiple responders. This approach is taken with many market research firms that conduct online surveys (P. McKerral, personal communication, June 10th, 1999). As with more traditional research methods, bogus answers are also a possibility with Internet studies, therefore social desirability scales or "checks" could be embedded in the questionnaire so that the researcher could sift through the data once collected and throw out any responses that seem implausible or faked.

Ethics and anonymity. Researchers wanting to use the Internet for data collection may face the problem of obtaining informed consent (King, 1996; Waskul & Douglass, 1996). While the Internet is technically a public domain, most users regard their online postings as relatively private and personal (Waskul & Douglass, 1996). Many researchers do not want to disrupt the natural flow of an online discussion group or chat room by asking for consent to observe the postings, take quotes, or otherwise use the contents of the postings for research purposes. The American Psychological Association (APA) has yet to set firm guidelines as to whether or not informed consent is necessary when obtaining research information from the Internet, although it is an issue they intend to address in the near future (for further information, see http://www.apa.org/ethics/). Nevertheless, researchers should be prudent and obtain consent from participants or list managers where possible or necessary, and should make every effort to protect the identities of the source(s) of the online information.

Once permission to post a project announcement has been obtained, the project description should be sent out to the list or provided to the link so as to approximate as closely as possible the traditional process for informed consent. However, some forms of research do not require active consent. If people are being recruited to fill out an anonymous survey, passive consent can often be assumed if they do, in fact, fill out the survey (American Psychological Association, 1992). For less obtrusive, naturalistic observational research, where obtaining informed consent may contaminate the data, nothing that can make the origin of the data identifiable should be included in the data set. As long as researchers protect the confidentiality or anonymity of the source of their material, or do the best they can to solicit informed participants, the ethics of online research should not be taken into question.

A final issue is that of *environmental conditions*. There is little control of environmental factors and extraneous variables when a person is accessing a survey on the Internet (Birnbaum, 1999; Michalak & Szabo, 1998). Some participants may be filling it out in the privacy and quiet of their home, while others may be in a crowded and noisy computer center. One way to control for environmental "noise" would be to specify or suggest, in the study instructions, conditions under which it should be conducted. While not all participants will follow the directions, it may help to eliminate or reduce error due to extraneous variables.

CONCLUSIONS

While it certainly can be argued that people who use the Internet do not adequately represent the overall population, it is clear that researchers can access a much larger, more varied, and thus more representative sample of potential participants through the Internet and the WWW than with the more "traditional" method of using university students as participants (Birnbaum, 1999). The use of the Internet to recruit participants not only increases the generalizability of most research findings, but opens up the door to cross-cultural and longitudinal research that would otherwise be too costly to conduct. With the testing, evaluation, and success that is currently being demonstrated with online participant recruitment and data collection, there is no reason to hesitate in capitalizing on the myriad of benefits the Internet affords researchers. Studies have demonstrated that not only can Internet sampling be used as a research method on its own, but it could also be used as an addition to the more "traditional" method as a means to increase sample size, to achieve more balanced demographic distribution, and to clarify and reinforce those results that are found in the lab (Birnbaum, 1999; Murray & Fisher, 1999; Smith & Leigh, 1997).

NOTE

1. The review was conducted in winter, spring and fall of 1999, using PsychINFO, MEDLINE and POPLINE. Keywords used in the search were Internet, technology, computer, web-based, computer-assisted, computerized, survey, research, online, and World Wide Web (WWW). Only articles published on or after 1990 were included in the review.

REFERENCES

American Psychological Association (1992). *Ethical Principles of Psychologists and Code of Conduct.* Retrieved January 21st, 2000 from the World Wide Web: http://www.apa.org/ethics/code.html#Principle C

Biesecker, L.G. & DeRenzo, E.G. (1995). Internet solicitation of research subjects for genetic studies. *American Journal of Human Genetics, 57,* 1255-1256.

Binik, Y.M., Mah, K., & Kiesler, S. (1999). Ethical issues in conducting sex research on the Internet. *Journal of Sex Research, 36,* 82-90.

Birnbaum, M.H. (1999). Testing critical properties of decision making on the Internet. *Psychological Science, 10,* 399-407.

Bourke, K. (1999). Net gains for research. *American Psychological Society Observer, 12,* 20-22.

Buchanan, T. & Smith, J.L. (1999). Using the Internet for psychological research: Personality testing on the World Wide Web. *British Journal of Psychology, 90,* 125-144.

Childress, C.A. & Asamen, J.K. (1998). The emerging relationship of psychology and the Internet: Proposed guidelines for conducting Internet intervention research. *Ethics & Behavior, 8,* 19-35.

Dahl, R.E. (1992). Response bias: Interactive effects of interview method, social desirability, evaluation of apprehension on self reported data. *Dissertation.*

Fawcett, J. & Buhle, E.L. (1995). Using the Internet for data collection: An innovative electronic strategy. *Computers in Nursing, 13,* 273-279.

GVU (1999). GVU's WWW User Surveys. Retrieved June 12th, 1999 from the World Wide Web <http://www.cc.gatech.edu/gvu/user_surveys/>

Hewson, C.M., Laurent, D., & Vogel, C.M. (1996). Proper methodologies for psychological and sociological studies conducted via the Internet. *Behavior Research Methods, Instruments, & Computers, 28,* 186-191.

Kelly, M.A. & Oldham, J. (1997). The Internet and randomized controlled trials. *International Journal of Medical Informatics, 47,* 91-99.

Kieley, J. M. (1996). CGI scripts: Gateways to World Wide Web power. *Behavior Research, Methods, Instruments, & Computers, 28,* 165-169.

King, S.A. (1996). Researching Internet communities: Proposed ethical guidelines for the reporting of the results. *The Information Society, 12,* 119-127.

Klemm, P. & Nolan, M.T. (1998). Internet cancer support groups: Legal and ethical issues for nurse researchers. *Oncology Nursing Forum, 25,* 673-676.

Lakeman, R. (1997). Using the Internet for data collection in nursing research. *Computers in Nursing, 5,* 269-275.

Lautenschlager, G.J. & Flaherty, V.L. (1990). Computer administration of questions: More desirable or more social desirability? *Journal of Applied Psychology, 75,* 310-314.

Lennon, S.J., Burns, L.D., & Rowold, K.L. (1995). Dress and human behavior research: Sampling, subjects, and consequences for statistics. *Clothing and Textiles Research Journal, 13,* 262-272.

Martin, J. (1999). http://aloha.acs.ohio-state.edu/videoc.html. November, 1999.

Mehta, R. & Sivadas, E. (1995). Comparing response rates and response content in mail versus electronic mail surveys. *Journal of Market Research Society, 37,* 429-439.

Michalak, E.E. & Szabo, A. (1998). Guidelines for Internet research: An update. *European Psychologist, 3,* 70-75.

Morrow, R.H. & McKee, A.J (1998). CGI scripts: A strategy for between-subjects experimental group assignment on the World-Wide Web. *Behavior Research Methods, Instruments, & Computers, 30,* 306-308.

Murray, D.M. & Fisher, J.D. (1999). Motorcycle safety gear use: A theoretical approach. Unpublished Manuscript.

Roberts, P., Scott, L., & Baluch, B. (1993). University: A venue for sex differences? *Psychological Reports, 72,* 833-834.

Sell, R.L. (1997). Research and the Internet: An e-mail survey of sexual orientation. *American Journal of Public Health, 87,* 297.

Smith, M.A. & Leigh, B. (1997). Virtual subjects: Using the Internet as an alternative source of subjects and research environment. *Behavior Research Methods, Instruments, & Computers, 29,* 496-505.

Stone, D.H. (1998). Research and the Internet. *Journal of Public Health Medicine, 20,* 111-112.

Subramanian, A.K., McAfee, A.T., & Getzinger, J.P. (1997). Use of the World Wide Web for multisite data collection. *Academic Emergency Medicine, 4,* 811-817.

Suchard, M.A., Hadfield, R., Elliot, T., & Kennedy, S. (1998). Beyond providing information: The Internet as a research tool in reproductive medicine. *Human Reproduction, 13,* 6-7.

Waskul, D. & Douglass, M. (1996). Considering the electronic participants: Some polemical observations on the ethics of online research. *The Information Society, 12,* 129-139.

Webster, J. & Compeau, D. (1996). Computer-assisted versus paper and pencil administration of questionnaires. *Behavior Research Methods, Instruments, & Computers, 28,* 567-576.

Whitener, E.M. & Klein, H.J. (1995). Equivalence of computerized and traditional research methods: The roles of scanning, social environment, and social desirability. *Computers in Human Behavior, 11,* 65-75.

Present Day Use of the Internet
for Survey-Based Research

J. E. Gonzalez

SUMMARY. This article argues that Internet-based survey research studies are presently limited in their utility. What many consider "classical" blunders in political polling that took place in the 1930s are used as a vehicle for describing parallel methodological errors that may occur with present-day use of the Internet. Without thoughtful protocols, Internet-based surveys are susceptible to these familiar errors, which limit their predictive utility. Tools such as e-mail, file transfers, and data and information access/retrieval should continue to be the primary role of Internet use. A model that articulates the use of Internet technology in survey research is offered for consideration. *[Article copies available for a fee from The Haworth Document Delivery Service: 1-800-HAWORTH. E-mail address: <getinfo@haworthpressinc.com> Website: <http://www.HaworthPress.com> © 2002 by The Haworth Press, Inc. All rights reserved.]*

KEYWORDS. Internet-based survey research methods

INTRODUCTION

In the none-too-distant past (1930s), what many now consider "classical" blunders in political polling predictions resulted when investiga-

J. E. Gonzalez, PhD, is Director, Social Science Research Center, Boise State University, 1910 University Drive, Boise, ID 83725 (jgonzal@ boisestate.edu).

[Haworth co-indexing entry note]: "Present Day Use of the Internet for Survey-Based Research." Gonzalez, J. E. Co-published simultaneously in *Journal of Technology in Human Services* (The Haworth Press, Inc.) Vol. 19, No. 2/3, 2002, pp. 19-31; and: *Using the Internet as a Research Tool for Social Work and Human Services* (ed: Goutham M. Menon) The Haworth Press, Inc., 2002, pp. 19-31. Single or multiple copies of this article are available for a fee from The Haworth Document Delivery Service [1-800-HAWORTH, 9:00 a.m. - 5:00 p.m. (EST). E-mail address: getinfo@haworthpressinc.com].

tors inadvertently drew biased samples; or introduced errors into their work due to their sampling procedures. In very public discussions that followed, political pollsters ultimately attributed the limited predictive power of their results to sampling error. For the decade that followed, sampling procedures and survey methods improved; but errors in political predictions persisted. Findings from a research council that was convened to study these errors, identified survey research methods and sampling errors as responsible for the limited utility of these political polls. Ross (1968) suggests instead, that the pollsters' undoing was caused by their insistence on predicting the outcome of future elections rather than on merely reporting the state of public opinion at some particular point in time, within some estimated margin of error.

This paper retraces the methodological errors of early pollsters, as the starting point for discussion of similar traps that may befall social scientists who are seduced by the glamour of the Internet and its potential usage as a research tool. As dominant a force as the Internet has become in our daily lives–it is not yet a universal constant–it is a powerful communication and information retrieval tool that is still only accessible to the "relative few." In the none-too-distant future, Internet connectivity may become so prevalent as to altogether replace telephone communication. Until then, however, a methodology for investigators who wish to use the Internet for research needs to be thoughtfully articulated. Otherwise, it is very likely that future Internet-based researchers will repeat the mistakes of the past.

POLLS–PROXIES FOR SOCIAL SCIENCE RESEARCH

One of the more interesting examples of a political poll that went awry was conducted by the *Literary Digest* in 1936. The results of that poll, published October 31st, 1936, predicted that Alf Landon, a Republican, would defeat the incumbent, Franklin D. Roosevelt, a Democrat. Although the poll results were close, the *Literary Digest* gave the win, 1,293,669 to 972,897, to Landon. By percentage points, it was predicted that Landon's 55% of ballots would beat Roosevelt's 41% of ballots. The *Literary Digest* reported that: "For nearly a quarter of a century, we have been taking Polls of the voters in the forty-eight States, and especially in Presidential years, and we have always merely mailed the ballots, counted and recorded those returned and let the people of the Nation draw their conclusions as to our accuracy. So far, we have been right in every Poll" (*Literary Digest*, October 1936, p. 5).

However, on Election Day, November 3, 1936–Franklin D. Roosevelt was reelected 32nd President, with a popular vote of 27,747,636; while Landon drew 16,679,543 votes (Southwick, 1984). By percentage points, Roosevelt's 61% (of the popular vote) compared to Landon's 37% was not remarkably dissimilar to the predicted proportions in the poll–just in favor of the wrong candidate. In the November 14th edition of the *Literary Digest,* the front-page headline read: "What Went Wrong with the Polls?" The editors wrote: "In 1920, 1924, 1928 and 1932, the *Literary Digest* Polls were right. Not only right in the sense that they showed the winner; they forecast the actual popular vote with such a small percentage of error (less than 1 percent in 1932) that newspapers and individuals everywhere heaped such phrases as 'uncannily accurate' and 'amazingly right' upon us" (*Literary Digest,* November 1936, p. 7).

What was the methodology used in that poll? Names for the poll came from: " . . . telephone books and lists of automobile owners . . . and more than ten million ballots were mailed out as had been done so before" (*Literary Digest,* November 1936, pp. 7-8). There were over two million ballots returned, but still, something went terribly wrong–So what? "So we were wrong" wrote the editors, " . . . although we did everything we knew to assure ourselves of being right. We conducted our Poll as we had always done, reported what we found, and have no alibis" (p. 7). This poll has been scrutinized by many, and is the source of valuable lessons learned on survey research methodology: a large sample does not necessarily offset errors; especially in the case where sample selection was biased.

Bennett (1980) wrote that the *Literary Digest* sample was inherently biased due to the sources of information that were used to build the database from which the sample was drawn. As reported by the *Literary Digest,* pollsters had used telephone books and automobile lists as primary sample sources; but subscribers to the *Literary Digest* made up a large part of the rest of the list. The author argues, " . . . only the relatively wealthy could afford to subscribe to magazines, own (or register) cars, or pay for a telephone. Such people, not hurt economically by the Depression, were the core of the Republican-party voting support for its economic programs" (Bennett, 1980, p. 67). The *Literary Digest* had unintentionally introduced social, political, and economic bias into their sample selection.

How did other pollsters fare that election year? Bennett notes that political pollsters such as Archibald Crossly, Elmo Roper, and George Gallup predicted the election correctly (1980). Bennett suggests that whereas other pollsters of the day may have generated better predictions, their sample sizes were too large and their research protocols included examples of other methodological errors. Bennett suggests that in these early polls, Gallup in particular, pollsters used sample sizes that were unnecessarily too large (N = 20,000+). Bennett notes that as the sample size increases, the standard error of measurement decreases; so at a 95% confidence interval, for specific sample sizes (N), standard error measurements (SE) are calculated as follows: for N = 94, SE ± 10.4; for N = 375, SE ± 5.1; for N = 1,500, SE ± 2.5; for N = 6,000, SE ± 1.3; for N = 24,000, SE ± .6; and for N = 96,000, SE ± .32 (1980, p. 71). Whereas a sufficiently large sample is important, there are obvious diminishing returns to very large samples. In the calculations above, a four-fold increase in sample size only results in a 50% decrease in the standard error of measurement. Instead, argues Bennett, carefully crafting the selection methodology generally produces better results.

By his own report, Gallup indicated that his final predictions favored Roosevelt by 55.7%, which, although correct, was still several percentage points fewer than in the actual election (1972). In describing what are now considered obvious errors in sampling procedures committed by the *Literary Digest,* Gallup adds that other factors may have influenced the outcome of that poll as well. For example, there was a substantial increase in the number of registered voters from lower income groups; groups which favored Roosevelt. As a result, the mailed ballot system method used in the poll may not have resonated well with these individuals, who presumably possessed lower educational levels (Gallup, 1972). According to Moore (1992), several additional important lessons were also learned as a result of these polls: sampling bias and response bias. In the first case, groups of individuals are systematically excluded from the sample; and in the second case, groups systematically exclude themselves from the study via non-response.

Another source of error may have also resulted from the timing factor. Apparently, the *Literary Digest* bulk-mailed their ballots in September; so any changes in voting trends that may have occurred towards the end of the campaign were not adequately reflected in the early tabulation of responses. Gallup's comments on the *Literary Digest* poll were not merely intended as academic observations of obvious errors. According to Moore (1992), Gallup had a substantial financial stake in the accuracy of his poll over that of the *Literary Digest.* Ten years later, in another famous election, pollsters such as Crossly, Roper, and Gallup all made substantial blunders in the 1948 Presidential election which were also publicly scrutinized. Many readers will no doubt recall the infamous photograph of newly elected President Harry S. Truman holding up a newspaper that in bold print read: "DEWEY DEFEATS TRUMAN" (*Chicago Tribune*, November, 1948). What went wrong in Gallup's poll for the *Chicago Tribune?*

According to Moore (1992), Gallup had been criticized by a Congressional Committee for not adopting a new "probability sampling" methodology that was becoming the vogue. Gallup responded that the costs associated with such a methodology would be too great and would only prove useful in critically close races. In hindsight, it turned out that the 1948 election was a critically close race. Later that year, a group of academics known as the "Social Science Research Council" convened a meeting, and asked the aforementioned pollsters to share their experiences. After a review of their material and much deliberation, the council issued a report, which suggested what might have gone wrong for these pollsters. In general, the council identified four commonalities among the pollsters: (1) all stopped polling too early; (2) all mishandled undecided voters; (3) none handled well the notion of the respondent's "intention to vote"; and (4) drawing probability-based samples continued to be a polling problem (Ross, 1968). Ross also notes that Wilfred J. Funk, the last editor of the *Literary Digest,* when asked about these pollsters, was quoted as saying: "I do not want to seem to be malicious, but I can't help but get a good chuckle out of this."

Moore writes that the great advances that had been made in legitimizing social science survey research methods " . . . were seriously undermined" (1992, p. 70) by the polls conducted in 1948. Moore noted that just like the *Literary Digest,* which went out of business shortly after the 1936 election, after the 1948 election many newspapers and magazines cancelled their polling services, and polling went out of favor. It was not until the 1960s that there was a resurgence in polls which were believed to have " . . . manipulative value"; otherwise, polling was relegated to " . . . linger in the realm of commerce" (Moore, 1992, p. 70).

Arguably, modern political polls are now conducted on carefully crafted (small) samples of individuals, right up until the very last days and moments prior to an election. Generally speaking, most polls are conducted via computer assisted telephone interview or CATI systems. But in recent years, the Internet has emerged as a technological tool that is being targeted for use in social science research. As testimony to the influence of this new survey research medium, even Dillman's classic work on survey research methods, *Mail and Telephone Surveys–The Total Design Method* (1978), has been updated in 2000, to include references on use of the Internet. With instant information and formidable "click-of-the-mouse" access to other Internet users via list-serves or chat rooms, it is easy to mistake these Internet features as a meaningful base from which to draw a sample for a research study. The section that follows describes the foibles of utilizing the Internet for serious research.

INTERNET USE, ACCESS, AND POSSIBLE SAMPLING ERRORS

To paraphrase a contemporary business slogan, the Internet and all things related are "moving at the speed of thought." The academic research-publication cycle, albeit thoughtful and deliberate, moves at "glacier-speed" when compared to the speeds found in development cycles for new technologies. The iterative nature of research, and the peer-review nature of academic scholarship, however, insures that methodological errors in research are constrained. With more reliance on the Internet for free information and discourse, those important safeguards may no longer hold. The phenomenal growth in the availability, use, and development of the Internet is leading many researchers to prematurely use it in place of probability-based sampling methods. Thoughtful protocols need to be developed lest Internet-based surveys become susceptible to the sampling errors of the past.

It is inevitable that by the time this sentence is printed, information as it relates to the Internet is outdated. Hallam (1998) notes that this is especially true when considering Internet-use statistics that are estimated to increase exponentially over time. Such projections are " . . . widely out of date by the time they are published" (Hallam, 1998, p. 241). Speed and growth are two attributes that best describe Internet use and application development. Since baseline information on these matters is important to the premise of this paper, a presentation of both academic press-based and Internet-based information on the development and use of the Internet follows.

It is noteworthy to recall that the U. S. Department of Defense computer-based e-mail system which was established in the late 1960s, laid the foundation for the present-day Internet (Kester, 1998; Hallam, 1998). Writes Hallam: "Initially developed in 1969 as a U. S. Department of Defense research project (ARPAnet), the origins of the Internet lay in the Cold War requirement for computer redundancy for national computer networks in the event of a hostile attack" (p. 243). A dedicated communication and research platform for the federal government is the backbone for today's Internet, which carries traffic from many more constituencies than what was originally intended (Braun & Claffy, 1995).

The Internet, according to Keller (1995), can also be defined as " . . . a set of voluntarily interconnected and interoperating networks that jointly support electronic mail, remote log-in and file transfer capabilities" (p. 35). Application protocols such as the WWW are " . . . built on top of the existing file transfer protocol, creating an easy-to-use interface typically based on point-and-click commands" (Keller, 1995, p. 30). The combination of partnerships, access protocols, and easy-to-use software are largely responsible for the present growth in the Internet.

Internet Use

According to Civille (1995), by mid-year 1994, there were an estimated 20 million individuals using the Internet in the U.S.; his estimates predicted a doubling of users to 40 million by the same time in 1995. A recent online posting (retrieved November 1999 from the World Wide Web: http://vactioner.com) suggested that there are presently 50 million users per day, who access the Internet from 80 countries; and by their estimates, an additional 2 million new users will come online each month. Whereas the number of users may not have increased as dramatically as first predicted by Civille, increases in Internet traffic volume are very large.

A recent online business posting (retrieved November 1999 from the World Wide Web: http://emarketer.com) estimated the following demographics for Internet users. Although these figures hint at the commercial profitability of the Internet, except for gender, they also suggest that users are not equally distributed across demographic categories. In Figure 1, please note that the racial background for the majority of users is White (87%), and that over 50% of users are below the age of 34.

Another recent online posting (retrieved November 1999 from the World Wide Web: http://rpcp.mit.edu) estimated that in November, 31 tera-bytes of information flowed across the Internet, which represents a phenomenal increase of 45% in the volume of traffic over that of the previous month of October. This phenomenal growth is largely being driven by Internet-based commerce. As early as 1994, Savetz estimated that commercial uses of the medium would account for " . . . about fifty percent of the Internet" (p. 306). Hallam (1994) found that computer host distribution figures for one month in 1994 showed nearly equal numbers of educational uses as commercial uses (Hallam found 1,326

FIGURE 1. Demographic Information of Internet Users

Age group	Pct:	Gender	Pct:	Race	Pct:
1-12	15 %	Female	49 %	White	87 %
13-17	14 %	Male	51 %	Black	7 %
18-34	29 %			Asian	5 %
35-54	31 %				
55+	12 %				

Retrieved November 1999 from the World Wide Web: http://emarketer.com

".com" registered domain names). Whereas industry figures boast an explosion in use of the Internet, other figures suggest that Internet use and access are not equally distributed.

Access

In the academic press, Civille (1995), using findings from the 1993 Current Population Survey (CPS) which included questions on home computer ownership and individual use, concluded that without government intervention a two-tiered society of information haves and have-nots will ultimately emerge. The 98.6 million households sampled in the 1993 CPS represented 69 million Americans with home personal computers. Further, reports Civille, 49% of households in the study had at least one member who used the Internet. The general attributes of Internet users represented in the study would be described as: economically middle to upper-class (defined as income greater than $30,000); living in metropolitan areas in the northeast or western states; likely to have a college degree; and to be an average age of 43.5 years (Civille, 1995).

Civille also noted that in addition to gender, education, and income differences in access to the Internet, there were also race and ethnicity differences, and metropolitan, non-metropolitan differences as well. According to the 1993 CPS, of Internet users both at work and at home, race and ethnic distributions were as follows: 12% White; 9.7% Asian; 6.7% Black; 4.8% Hispanic; and less than 1% Native American; also 20.4% of Internet users were in metropolitan areas, compared to 17.2% in rural areas. Interestingly, Civille also compared personal computer users in the working class town of Flint, Michigan to the college town of Ann Arbor, Michigan, and found only 5.4% of households in Flint had

Internet use, compared to 26.6% of Internet users in households in Ann Arbor.

These demographics, gleaned from older CPS data, paint a different portrait of users than that described by commercial statistics. Kester's (1998) profile of Internet users, for example, is similar to the CPS reports. Since the Internet was originally established by the U.S. military and is operated primarily by government-funded universities and businesses, it is no surprise that it " . . . is used by an overwhelmingly white, male cadre of professionals and intellectuals who are the beneficiaries of a highly developed system of technical education, and of an information economy whose global impact has been profoundly divisive" (Kester, 1998, p. 227). One could argue that drawing an unbiased Internet-based sample for research is therefore quite difficult, given these user profile figures. A larger problem resides in the fact that the Internet is so very large that its actual size can only be estimated; thus further exacerbating sampling problems in terms of standard error calculations.

For example, during a one-month period in 1992, Braun and Claffy conducted an analysis of NSF network traffic, and tracked over one million network pairs of information across their monitoring system. Their monitoring system utilized a sampling mechanism that collected every 50th packet of information that was exchanged across the 21,000 networks in the NSF at that time. The authors noted that it was impossible to assess with certainty whether their sample of exchange pairs of information was representative of the total Internet traffic for that time period (Braun & Claffy, 1995). This example illustrates that the size of the Internet is so vast that the whole of the Internet cannot be assessed; and therefore neither can the validity of an Internet sample.

Possible Sampling Errors

Can a sample of individuals be drawn from the Internet? The answer of course is yes–a non-probability sample. Beginning with the caveat that users need "to be socially responsible," Barrett (1997) writes that the Internet itself can be used to easily find people. The best examples offered by Barrett are "white pages" or "directories" that are compiled by individuals or companies. Munger et al. (1999) note that "at the moment, there are more than twenty thousand newsgroups online with an estimated ten million Usenet users" (p. 42). Finding newsgroups is as easy as utilizing a search engine to identify an index of newsgroups.

The authors note that *www.liszt.com/news*, for example, is a great starting place (Munger et al., 1999, p. 44). For accessing a group of individuals, Barrett suggests tapping into Usenet groups or listservs. But the one method that Barrett considers "insidious" is actually the best method to draw a sample of Internet users–contact Internet Service Providers (ISPs) for permission to access their users.

The non-random nature of these types of samples (sampling bias) are further complicated by response bias. Brehm writes: "If survey respondents are underrepresentative of the population, then one loses the ability to generalize from surveys to the population" (p. 23). He also notes that: "Internal (and external) validity is at risk if the attitudes and characteristics of respondents differ from nonrespondents" (Brehm, 1993, p. 23). In his work, Brehm found evidence of response bias in age, gender, race and education.

Regarding age, Brehm notes that: "There are good a priori reasons to be concerned about how surveys represent particular age groups. The age of the respondent may be related to how busy that respondent is, how available the respondent would be during particular hours, how amenable a respondent would be to participating in a survey or how healthy a respondent might be" (p. 26). In regards to gender Brehm notes that: "There are good reasons to suspect that surveys might undercount men. Although the proportion of women in the workforce has been rising, there are still more working men than women" (p. 30). Lastly, Brehm notes that race and education are also affected as is place of residence. Based on the work of Kalton, a recognized statistician, Brehm then describes the necessary calculations for correcting non-response bias in sample means for univariate estimates and for multivariate relationships.

In the immediate future Internet-based research will likely be a seamless transaction. From start to finish, the Internet will be an extraordinary tool for research, from instrumentation and sampling to interactive dissemination of research findings. Data capture and database development for statistical analysis is presently available via Web page interface. Application software is also becoming available that will allow end-users to query data reports for more specific detail or to mine data directly from the author's database. But until there is universal access to the Internet–Internet-based surveys will likely be biased by including only particular groups of individuals and excluding all others. So what is the present-day use of the Internet for research?

DISCUSSION

The Internet is a powerful tool that will deliver as promised, when its use is more universal; but in the meantime, hopeful optimism and enthusiasm must give way to practical considerations. Presently, the Internet can appropriately be used to conduct literature reviews, to correspond with colleagues, and to exchange data files. Some institutional data is also available online to users, with query capability forecast for the near future. There are applications, however, that are still largely proprietary in nature. In Figure 2, it is suggested that the present-day utility of the Internet is that of a supportive role in survey research. In the future, data collection activity, interactive data manipulation, and dissemination of information will be an integral feature of the Internet, and will perhaps in time displace other forms of survey research.

What about the notion of using the Internet as a medium for survey research? This paper has presented information arguing against the use of Internet-based survey research based upon unequal access and use of the Internet by select groups of individuals. However, if a researcher chooses this medium, special care must be taken when developing the database of Internet addresses from which to draw a sample. To the extent possible, data must be verified against a known demographic profile. Commercial research houses are becoming available and will provide ready access to lists of Internet users. But better yet, wait a bit longer for the access and use of the technology to become universal.

FIGURE 2. Model for Present and Future Use of the Internet for Survey-Based Research

Present Use	Future Use
For: Face-to-face; mail-based; and telephone-based surveys	**For:** Internet-based surveys
Primary Support Includes: Literature Reviews	**Primary Support Includes:** Literature Reviews
	Internet Support Includes: E-mail with Colleagues Data File Transfer
	Plus: Integrated Research Protocols Data Collection Activity Interactive Data Manipulation Dissemination of Findings

A Research Protocol

Presently, the Internet can also be used to complement traditional survey media. It may be used to reach certain populations of users, but such a study can only produce credible results in combination with probability-based sampling methodology. For example, an organization can only expect accurate results from a survey of its members by Internet, if all members of the organization have Internet addresses. Alternatively, if the proportion of Internet addresses is known, then an Internet-based survey to a sub-sample of individuals can accompany a mail-based survey and yield representative results. Utilizing traditional survey research methods and allowing respondents the opportunity to respond via the Internet can obtain the best survey results.

In the meantime, however, researchers should scour the academic-press for critique of new methodologies on the use of the Internet in survey research (Dillman, 2000). Perhaps one day, the classic Cochran (1977) formula for estimating sampling error will also be updated for use with Internet-based survey research data. And as Hallam notes, in order to stay abreast of Internet development, researchers should become active online Internet participants (1998). However, rather than posting Internet addresses that will be obsolete or "404-ed" by the time this paper is printed, instead readers are encouraged to explore the Internet for online information on items discussed in this paper: use, access, online surveys, sampling procedures, and additional materials on Internet-based research.

REFERENCES

Barrett, D. J. (1997). *NetResearch: Finding information online.* Sebastopol, CA: Songline Studios.

Bennett, W. L. (1980). *Public opinion in American politics.* New York: Harcourt Brace Jovanovich.

Braun, H. & Claffy, K. (1995). "Network analysis issues for a public Internet." In B. Kahin and J. Keller (Eds.), *Public access to the Internet* (pp. 350-377). Cambridge, MA: The MIT Press.

Brehm, J. (1993). *The phantom respondents.* Ann Arbor, MI: The University of Michigan Press.

Chicago Tribune. (November, 1948). "DEWEY DEFEATS TRUMAN."

Civille, R. (1995). "The Internet and the poor." In B. Kahin and J. Keller (Eds.), *Public access to the Internet* (pp. 175-207). Cambridge, MA: The MIT Press.

Cochran, W. (1977). *Sampling techniques.* New York: John Wiley & Sons.

Dillman, D. A. (1978). *Mail and telephone surveys–The total design method.* New York: Wiley.

Dillman, D. A. (2000). *Mail and Internet surveys: The tailored design method.* New York: Wiley.

Gallup, G. (1972). *The sophisticated poll watcher's guide.* Princeton: Princeton Opinion Press.

Hallam, S. (1998). "Misconduct on the information highway: Abuse and misuse of the Internet." In R. N. Stichler and R. Hauptman (Eds.), *Ethics, information and technology readings* (pp. 241-254). Jefferson, NC: McFarland & Co., Inc.

Keller, J. (1995). "Public Access issues: An introduction." In B. Kahin and J. Keller (Eds.), *Public access to the Internet* (pp. 34-45). Cambridge, MA: The MIT Press.

Kester, G. H. (1998). "Access denied: Information policy and the limits of liberalism." In R. N. Stichler and R. Hauptman (Eds.), *Ethics, information and technology readings* (pp. 207-230). Jefferson, NC: McFarland & Co., Inc.

Literary Digest (October 31, 1936; pp. 5-6). "Landon, 1,293,669; Roosevelt, 972,897."

Literary Digest (November 14, 1936; pp. 7-8). "What went wrong with the polls?"

Moore, D. W. (1992). *The Superpollseters.* New York: Four Walls Eight Windows.

Munger, D., Anderson, D., Benjamin, B., Busiel, C., & Paredes-Holt, B. (1999). *Researching online.* New York: Longman.

Ross, I. (1968). "What happened?" In *The loneliest campaign.* Retrieved November 1999 from the World Wide Web: http://www.whistlestop.org.

Savetz, K. (1994). *Your Internet consultant: The FAQs of life online.* Indianapolis, IN: SAMS Publishing.

Southwick, L. H. (1984). *Presidential also rans and running mates, 1788-1980.* Jefferson, NC: McFarland.

Collecting Data via the Internet:
The Development and Deployment
of a Web-Based Survey

Joel Epstein
W. Dean Klinkenberg

SUMMARY. This report discusses the process of developing and deploying an Internet-based study that sought to replicate the results of a traditionally administered questionnaire. We present data on the characteristics of respondents, hit and completion rates, and the effectiveness of a dozen different methods of advertising the survey. Overall, we were very successful in soliciting a gay and lesbian sample of Internet-users and collected one of the largest samples for a Web-based survey to date. Publicity methods that addressed the target audience's specific interests were far more effective than broader advertising methods. *[Article copies available for a fee from The Haworth Document Delivery Service: 1-800-HAWORTH. E-mail address: <getinfo@haworthpressinc.com> Website: <http://www.HaworthPress.com> © 2002 by The Haworth Press, Inc. All rights reserved.]*

KEYWORDS. Internet, survey, process

Joel Epstein, PhD, and W. Dean Klinkenberg, PhD, are affiliated with the University of Missouri School of Medicine, Missouri Institute of Mental Health, Saint Louis, MO.

Address correspondence to: Dr. Joel Epstein, Missouri Institute of Mental Health, 5400 Arsenal Street, Saint Louis, MO 63139 (E-mail: epsteinj@mimh.edu).

[Haworth co-indexing entry note]: "Collecting Data via the Internet: The Development and Deployment of a Web-Based Survey." Epstein, Joel, and W. Dean Klinkenberg. Co-published simultaneously in *Journal of Technology in Human Services* (The Haworth Press, Inc.) Vol. 19, No. 2/3, 2002, pp. 33-47; and: *Using the Internet as a Research Tool for Social Work and Human Services* (ed: Goutham M. Menon) The Haworth Press, Inc., 2002, pp. 33-47. Single or multiple copies of this article are available for a fee from The Haworth Document Delivery Service [1-800-HAWORTH, 9:00 a.m. - 5:00 p.m. (EST). E-mail address: getinfo@haworthpressinc.com].

Only recently have researchers been using the Internet as a means for collecting psychological data. The American Psychological Society compiles a list of active Internet-based data collection efforts (psych. hanover.edu/APS/exponnet.html) that covers numerous domains and dozens of different studies. Despite its growing popularity, articles published on web-based data collection are still relatively rare (Pettit, 1999).

Because the field is so new, the literature that describes Internet-based studies often devotes entire sections to discussions of the benefits and problems associated with such data collection efforts. Problems mentioned include sampling issues, lack of control over the experimental environment, and data integrity and security. Benefits mentioned include access to difficult-to-reach populations, ease of data collection, and greater disclosure from respondents (Epstein & Klinkenberg, 2000).

The handful of published Internet data collection studies has used a striking variety of methodologies. Some researchers have simply e-mailed questionnaires to systematically collected e-mail addresses (Anderson & Gansneder, 1995; Swoboda, Muhlberger, Weitkunat, & Schneeweiss, 1997). Others have posted surveys designed to collect demographic, attitudinal, and behavioral data (Kaye & Johnson, 1999; Nicholson, White, & Duncan, 1998). More sophisticated Internet research involves comparing data collected online to results published in the literature (Michalak, 1998; Stones & Perry, 1997) or to traditionally collected laboratory samples (Pasveer & Ellard, 1998; Davis, 1999). Finally, researchers have used theoretical approaches to validate the data they collect over the Internet (Buchanan & Smith, 1999).

This article seeks neither to discuss the pros and cons of Internet-based data collection nor to analyze the results of such a data collection effort. Rather, we will describe the process of developing and deploying an Internet survey and draw conclusions as to the success of our methods.

Our initial goal was to replicate a study of HIV risk behavior which demonstrated that intentions to use a condom were inversely correlated with perceived attractiveness of a potential sexual partner (Agocha & Cooper, 1999). The original study data were collected via a traditional paper and pencil survey using a heterosexual undergraduate sample. For our replication, however, we sought to solicit a gay and lesbian sample using the Internet. Results of the success of replicating the original findings are discussed elsewhere (Klinkenberg, Epstein, Scandell, & Faulkner, 2000).

QUESTIONNAIRE DEVELOPMENT AND DEPLOYMENT

Before beginning our study, we sought approval from our University's Institutional Review Board (IRB). We expected that our study would be exempt from full review, because we were not collecting any information that could personally identify an individual respondent. Our IRB had several questions related to the collection of IP addresses and the use of cookies. Members of the IRB mistakenly believed that cookies and IP addresses could be used to personally identify a respondent. After we corrected their misperception, they approved the project but still required us to post information in the online consent form explaining cookies and IP addresses to participants. Ironically, the IRB approved our project as minimal risk requiring only "verbal" consent from participants, further demonstrating that Internet-based research is still a very unfamiliar realm to most IRBs. We ended up posting an electronic consent form, and participants were required to click on the "I consent" button before they could access the questionnaire.

Once IRB approval was obtained, we were able to begin the process of translating the original survey into a format suitable for presentation on the Internet. We ended up coding the entire survey by hand using a simple text processor. Although there are numerous high-end software packages available for creating HTML documents, we chose not to use them because they typically create documents which contain unnecessary code which is difficult to debug.

Questionnaire Content

The final questionnaire contained 27 demographic questions including items such as age, gender, sexual orientation, relationship status, and sexual history. Following the demographic questions, the survey presented a person's photograph and a brief biographical sketch. Heterosexual respondents were presented a photograph of an opposite-gender individual; respondents who identified as gay, lesbian, bisexual, or "unsure" of their sexual orientation were presented a photograph of a same-gender individual. Participants were randomly assigned to view a photograph of a highly attractive or less attractive individual (see Epstein, Klinkenberg, Wiley, & McKinley, 2000 for a discussion of how the photographs were selected). Additionally, the biographical sketch was manipulated to describe the individual as having either a high, medium, or low amount of previous sexual experience. All other information in the biographical sketch was held constant. We therefore had a 2 (physical attractiveness) by 3 (sexual history) design with participants randomly assigned to one of the six different conditions.

The main content of the questionnaire was contained in 43 attitudinal questions, asking respondents to rate how attractive they found the presented person to be, how likely they would want to be in a relationship with that person, and how likely they would be to practice safer sex with the person. Respondents who did not indicate they were heterosexual also received 10 additional items on internalized homophobia.

Almost all data collected was in the form of Likert-type questions. Very little use was made of free-text entry. Before respondents could proceed to a subsequent page in the survey, all missing answers were flagged and all free-text data were error-checked. In this way, data collected were assured to contain no missing values and to be within a prescribed range.

Both assigned variables (i.e., attractiveness and sexual history) were set as soon as a respondent consented to participate in the questionnaire. In this way, backtracking through the survey would not lead to reassignment of experimental condition.

Questionnaire Debugging

Once the survey had been completely coded (approximately two months), we began a process of debugging. Our first step was to go through the survey several times and make sure that the code was working correctly. For example, we had to insure that the phrasing of the questions changed based on the respondent's gender and sexual orientation. Then, unlike other studies in which submitted data are e-mailed to the investigator, our data were placed directly into a database. For security purposes, this database was located under a directory that was inaccessible from the Internet. We conducted numerous tests to insure that the data entered on the web site actually matched the data that were entered into the database. Doing this crosscheck allowed us to catch any last-minute coding errors. Finally, and definitely most problematic, came the process of checking the survey across different software packages and computer platforms. Not all browsers handle HTML coding the same way and, therefore, minor changes were required to insure that the survey appeared as identical as possible across a wide variety of computers and browsers.

Publicizing the Questionnaire

One aspect of our investigation was the analysis of which methods were most effective in bringing participants to our survey. We identified 12 different methods of publicizing our web site. In order to track which methods were most successful, we used a different URL for each. For example, the URL in our magazine advertisement was *http://www. aboutsex.org/survey* and the URL listed on search engines was *http://www. aboutsex.org/rating*. As much as possible, we tried to keep the content of the advertisements consistent across all methods of recruiting. See Table 1 for a listing of the methods of publicizing the survey.

RESULTS

As previously mentioned, the data relating to the replication of the original study is discussed elsewhere (Klinkenberg et al., 2000). This article focuses primarily on the effectiveness of the methods of publicizing the survey and other qualitative findings.

Participants

Previous Internet studies (Buchanan & Smith, 1999; Pasveer & Ellard, 1998; Richard, 2000) have described a data screening procedure that attempted to identify repeat users. This methodology examined the user's Internet Protocol (IP) number and removed any data that came from identical IP numbers. This procedure, however, does not necessarily rid the final data set of repeated users. Most Internet users are not connected directly to the Internet. Instead, they either dial-up a service provider (e.g., America On-line, Earthlink, etc.) or connect via a small to mid-size network (e.g., Intranet) which is in turn connected to the Internet. In either case, each time a user initiates a new Internet session, an IP number is randomly assigned from a pool of numbers available to that network or service provider. Therefore, duplicate IP numbers in the researcher's database do not necessarily mean that a single user has entered data twice. More likely, a different user has been randomly assigned a number that a previous participant had been assigned. Conversely, a single participant is unlikely to be assigned the same IP number on multiple times s/he connects to the Internet, further making examination of IP numbers an ineffective strategy for identifying repeat users.

For our study, we utilized a different method to identify repeat users. Each time someone visited our survey, a small text file (called a cookie) was written to their computer's hard-drive. The programming in our

TABLE 1. Methods of Publicizing the Survey

Method	Description
Newsgroups	Sent messages to 40 different newsgroups that discussed gay, lesbian or bisexual content.
Search Engine	Paid $25.00 to a company to have our survey listed on over 1000 different Internet search engines.
Meta Tags	Included coding in the survey's programming that would allow web spiders to index our site.
Spam E-mail	Paid $359.00 to a company to send 500,000 unsolicited e-mail messages about our survey.
Web Page Owners	Identified 137 web sites devoted to gay or lesbian issues and asked their webmasters to link to our survey.
Banner Advertisement	Paid $400.00 for a banner advertisement to appear 50,000 times at a prominent gay/lesbian-oriented web site.
Print Advertisement	Paid $410.00 for a one- and one-half inch advertisement in a national gay/lesbian magazine.
Listserve	Sent messages to the owners of 57 gay/lesbian-oriented listserves asking them to mention our survey in a posting.
Stickers	Distributed approximately 1000 stickers in local gay and lesbian bars advertising our survey.
Referrals	Sent approximately 75 messages to friends, family, and colleagues asking for help recruiting participants.
Opt-In E-mails	Spent $434.00 for a company to send 2168 e-mails to individuals who had previously indicated an interest in completing psychological surveys online.
Radio Spots	Had public service announcements air for free during a gay/lesbian talk show on a local public-access radio station.

survey then examined that cookie and determined whether or not that computer had visited the survey before. We then examined all database entries for which the cookie was greater than one. Of course, simply removing all these cases could result in improper exclusion. For example, both a terminal at a campus computing lab, or a computer shared by partners at the same household could conceivably have a cookie status greater than one without representing multiple entries from a single individual. Therefore, we only removed cases from the database when the cookie status was greater than one and the responses were clearly identical to other entries in the database (i.e., gender, orientation, age, etc.). Although this procedure is not able to screen hoax or disingenuous responses, it does represent a more accurate method of screening the data than examination of IP numbers.

Our data collection period lasted for approximately eight months. During this time 1,434 surveys were completed. It should be noted, however, that 77.8% of the data (1,116 surveys) were completed within the first month of the data collection period, the time period during which our recruiting efforts were most intensive. After screening all returned surveys as indicated above, we were left with a total of 1,386 usable responses. The 48 surveys discarded represented only 3% of the total data collected.

One thousand sixty-six (76%) participants were male, 695 identified themselves as gay or lesbian (50%), and the average age of all participants was 33.84. See Table 2 for a summary of the participants' gender and sexual orientation. One thousand eighty-seven (86%) participants were white and there were less than 4% each of African Americans, Asians, Native Americans, Latinos, and those indicating "Other" as a racial category. On average, participants had completed nearly 15 years of schooling.

Web Log Tracking Results

In addition to the results obtained by formally analyzing the data collected by the survey, we also gathered data from a software package which tracks all activity on the web site. These data are compiled automatically and do not require any intervention from either the researchers or the participants. Any time an Internet user typed our survey's address into his/her browser, our tracking software recorded information about that request. Although this software collects a wide variety of information, we were most interested in when and from where the requests were made and the overall ratio of visits to the site versus completed questionnaires.

During the data collection period, the first page of our survey (the introduction page) was viewed 4,663 times. Given that 1,434 completed questionnaires were received in our database, 3,229 views (or 69%) did not result in a survey completion. As can be seen in Table 3, individuals dropped out of the survey at a variable rate throughout the survey, with most drop-outs coming before any data were actually collected and a nearly equal percentage coming on the questionnaire page (which represented the bulk of the survey items).

A majority of our participants (86%) came from the United States. Approximately 2% of all participants came from Canada and 1% each came from Australia, Mexico, France, United Kingdom, and Germany. A total of 63 different countries were represented and included such

TABLE 2. Participants' Gender and Sexual Orientation

		Male		TG: F->M		Female		TG: M->F		Total
	Gay	**599**	86%	**1**	<1%	**95**	14%	**0**	0%	**695**
		57%	43%	14%	<1%	30%	7%	0%	0%	50%
	Bi	**159**	63%	**2**	1%	**89**	35%	**1**	<1%	**251**
Orientation		15%	11%	28%	<1%	28%	6%	100%	<1%	18%
	Hetero	**263**	68%	**1**	<1%	**125**	32%	**0**	0%	**389**
		25%	19%	14%	<1%	39%	9%	0%	0%	28%
	Unsure	**38**	75%	**3**	6%	**10**	20%	**0**	0%	**51**
		3%	3%	43%	<1%	3%	1%	0%	0%	4%
	Total	**1059**	76%	**7**	<1%	**319**	23%	**1**	<1%	**1386**

(Gender spans the Male, TG: F->M, Female, TG: M->F, Total columns.)

notes:
TG = transgender
For each cell, the bold number in the upper left corner represents the frequency, the number immediately to the right of that represents the percentage for that gender, the number below the frequency represents the percentage for that sexual orientation, and the number in the bottom right-hand corner represents the overall percentage.

TABLE 3. Drop-Outs Throughout the Survey

Page	**Number of views**	**# of Drop-Outs**	**% Drop-Out from Previous Page**
Intro	4663	0	--
Consent	3326	1337	28.67
Demographics	2544	782	23.51
Questionnaire	2058	486	19.10
Completion	1434**	624	30.32

** This represents the total number of completed surveys including duplicate submissions.

small nations as Bhutan, Zimbabwe, and Luxembourg. These data are not based on self-report, but rather our web tracking software's analysis of the origin of each request.

Other web log data revealed that almost 14.5% of all participants used AOL and nearly 4.75% used WebTV as their Internet service provider. The remainder of the users had various other Internet service providers. Tuesdays were the survey's busiest days and the time periods between 11:00 a.m.-11:59 a.m. and 8:00 p.m.-midnight local time were the survey's most active periods. Although approximately 26% of all visitors spent less than one minute with our survey, approximately 22.5% spent over 19 minutes.

Qualitative Results

The last question of our survey asked participants to enter any comments they might have. Of the 1,386 usable questionnaires, 416 (30%) included comments. Additionally, we received numerous e-mails regarding the survey. Taken together, these comments were nearly evenly distributed in terms of their praise and criticism for the survey. Of the negative comments, many included criticisms that the survey items did not clearly define "sex" as well as a concern that the survey items failed to address the specific concerns of bisexual people. Positive comments ranged from participants wanting to see results of the survey to others indicating that it helped them think more critically about their own risky sexual behaviors. In addition to comments regarding the questionnaire, we also received an amazing amount of self-disclosures. See Table 4 for a sampling of participants' comments.

Effectiveness of Publicity Methods

There are numerous ways to assess the effectiveness of publicizing our survey. See Table 5 for an overview of these data. The simplest method examines the number of times Internet users made a request (known as a "hit") for each URL representing the different publicity methods. Nearly 1,000 hits came from users who had seen our survey posted on other web pages. This represented 200 more hits than the next most effective method: announcements on listserves. Junk e-mail represented the third most effective method of obtaining hits. No hits were received via including meta-tags in the survey's programming. Radio PSAs and distribution of advertising stickers at gay bars brought the next fewest hits respectively. We also tracked users who reached our survey by means other than those that we specifically advertised. Although it was a relatively small number, people who did not use an advertised URL to reach our survey obtained over 100 hits. In all likelihood, these people saw one of our ads somewhere else and just remembered the first part of the URL (i.e., *www.aboutsex.org*).

Although analysis of hit frequencies reveals which methods were most successful in bringing users to our survey, it does not tell us whether or not the users completed the survey. To obtain this statistic, we looked at which method of publicity resulted in the most surveys

TABLE 4. Comments About the Questionnaire

Negative Comments:

General Complaints
- "A trifle longish."
- "I had some computer problems."
- "I believe that some of the questions seem quite ambiguous."
- "Just another peek-a-boo type survey by people with nothing better to do."

Believability of Manipulation
- "I don't believe the person in the photo is 32."
- "You tell us he's had one sexual partner. Does that mean it is the truth or are we supposed to trust the guy or not?"

Lack of specificity for the term "sex"
- "You need to define what constitutes sex."
- "Is mutual masturbation classed as sex, is oral?"
- "Please define what you mean by sex."

Homosexuality is not the same as bisexuality
- "As a bisexual person, I identify as bisexual, not gay. A few of the questions seemed to lump the two together."
- "It is clear to me that the people who created this questionnaire don't understand bisexuality at all."
- "I find the questionnaire does little to help bisexual people feel more at home with themself and thank goodness I am not transgender or attracted to them sexually because it does not seem to cater to them and their identity or desires."

No Spam (unsolicited e-mail)
- "Remove me."
- "I was not particularly happy to be spammed about this questionnaire."

Positive Comments:

General Praise
- "Great questionnaire"
- "Very interesting"
- "Very well thought out"

Helpful
- "I thought it was interesting and even kinda educational."
- "Excellent question wording. Even the act of asking these questions installs a self-realization of your sexual habits."
- "Really tough questions to answer in that they made me look deeper into myself than I'm used to doing."
- "Makes you think of how much risk we take for sex."

Want to see the results
- "Would like to see the results"
- Many participants also included phone numbers or e-mails so that they could be informed as to the survey's results.

Other Comments:

Regarding the individuals pictured in the questionnaire
- "I find her so utterly unattractive."
- "Not my type"
- "I would not have sex with him under any circumstances–I do have an age limit."
- "I would like to meet the lady in the picture or exchange phone numbers."
- "Very interesting guy and would love to have him as a friend."

Self-disclosures
- "I did attempt suicide trying to suppress my homosexuality."
- "Wife can't handle I will have sex with men."
- "Because of my upbringing, my parents cannot know about my sexuality."
- "I am still a virgin."
- "I came out to my wife 2 years ago."
- "I love being gay."

TABLE 5. Hits and Completions by Publicity Method

Source	Cost	Hits	Completions	Hits / Completions	Not Hetero	Completions / Not Hetero
Banner Ad	400	272	90	33.1	89	98.9
Listserve Requests	0	794	193	24.3	189	97.9
Meta Tags	0	0	0	0	0	0
Newsgroup	0	294	46	15.6	44	95.7
Opt-In E-mail	434	550	148	26.9	40	27.0
Other	0	114	78	68.4	45	57.7
Our Referrals	0	418	182	43.5	133	73.1
Print Ad	410	212	106	50.0	101	95.3
Radio	0	40	5	12.5	4	80.0
Search Engine	25	170	16	9.4	10	62.5
Spam Mail	359	755	177	23.4	36	20.3
Stickers	30	50	11	22.0	10	90.9
Web Page Owners	0	994	334	33.6	296	88.6
TOTALS	1658	4663	1386		997	

completed. Again, advertisements on other people's web pages and postings to listserves proved to be the two most effective methods respectively. The third most effective method was via our requests to colleagues and friends. Radio PSAs and stickers resulted in the fewest number of completions.

Another way of looking at the effectiveness of the methods of publicizing the survey is to look at the ratio of hits to completions. This is, in a way, a method of gauging the relevancy of the site to the participants' interests. Surprisingly, users who came to the survey independent of any of our advertising methods represented the best hit to completion ratio. The magazine advertisement and our referrals were the next best methods. Advertisements via search engines, radio, and newsgroups had the poorest hit to completion ratios.

Finally, we analyzed the effectiveness of each publicity method at bringing members of the target audience (gay, lesbian, bisexual, and transgendered people) to our survey. For each method we computed the percent of surveys that were completed by individuals who did not indicate a heterosexual orientation. Although most of the methods of publicity resulted in nearly three-quarters or greater of all respondents being non-heterosexual, both spam mail and opt-in e-mailings were remarkably poor (less than 30%) at bringing members of our target audience to the survey.

CONCLUSIONS

Participants

Nearly 70% of all visits to our site did not result in a survey being completed. This large figure could be due to the survey not matching participants' expectations, or a general unwillingness to spend the time required to answer all the questions. It is even possible that some people returned to the site later to complete the survey. Nevertheless, our study represents one of the largest samples of participants collected via the Internet for a psychologically oriented survey to date.

As with other Internet samples, however, our participants were, for the most part, from the United States, White, and well-educated. Therefore, generalization of our sample to different populations may not be appropriate. Another significant sampling issue is the fact that a sizable proportion of our participants did come from outside the United States. Not only is it difficult to translate various demographic variables (e.g., education, income, etc.), it is unclear if the specific terminology of our survey (i.e., homosexuality and safer sex) translates to similar concepts and practices in other countries. This, of course, is not an issue unique to our Internet study and will be an ongoing issue for future research.

Qualitative Issues

It is abundantly clear that a sizable proportion of our participants were passionate about the issues raised by our survey. Nearly one-quarter of all participants spent nearly 20 minutes or more answering our questions. It is gratifying to know that many participants were truly appreciative of our efforts and even stated that they gained some insight into their own behavior in the process of completing the survey. Even the criticisms of our work are appreciated because they help us to design better survey questions for future studies. Although the self-disclosures participants made were instructive, a surprising number of comments were actually requests for help or assistance. Not only did several participants ask specific questions relating to homosexuality, a review of the web tracking logs reveals that several participants reached our site by typing "gay and lesbian advice" into a search engine.

Clearly, our survey was not designed as an intervention. Nevertheless, having the questionnaire on the Internet seemed to have made us "instant experts." We tried to answer all e-mails as promptly as possible and provide referrals when necessary. However, in the future, researchers may need to explicitly state that the purpose of their investigation is to collect data and not to provide services. Additionally, it would be both thoughtful and beneficial to provide a list of links to relevant information on the Internet. Finally, researchers should strive to make the results of their survey available on their web site as soon as possible.

Publicity Methods

Methods that specifically targeted gay and lesbian audiences were clearly more effective than broader advertising efforts. Posts to listserves and links on other people's web pages helped bring participants to our site because they were personally relevant. Conversely, junk e-mails were not as effective because they did not reach our target audience. It is conceivable, however, that a mailing via an opt-in list could be effective if the list was specifically focussed. For this project, however, we were unable to find a customized list targeting a gay and lesbian audience.

It is interesting that the "other" category provided us with the best hit/completion ratio. To review, individuals in this group reached our site not via any of the publicized methods, but rather by typing our base URL directly. It is likely that these individuals had remembered our site from some other source and therefore had a specific interest in seeing our survey. This result attests to the fact that users do not typically browse the Internet aimlessly, but specifically seek out personally relevant information.

Both the magazine advertisement and the banner ad provided roughly equivalent results. What is notable about this is that while the banner ad allowed for direct access to our site (via a click of the mouse), the print advertisement required participants to either memorize the URL or write it down for later reference. The higher level of motivation required to remember the URL and later access the web site may account for the higher completion ratio for people recruited from the print ad versus the banner ad.

Given the success of the print advertisement, it may seem odd that our radio ads were not very successful. Although our site was promoted on a local gay and lesbian talk-show, the listenership, while undetermined, is admittedly rather small. We had limited funds with which to complete our study and a future investigation might find interesting results analyzing the effectiveness of advertising via traditional broadcast media.

There are numerous companies advertising on the Internet that promise to boost traffic to users' sites by providing metatag programming and high ratings in search engines. Results of our investigation indicate that such efforts are probably not worth the money or effort. There are so many web sites that it is easy for any one site to get overlooked. Clearly, the best publicity methods are those that personalize the content to the target audience.

In summary, we were able to design, develop, and implement an Internet-based research project with an experimental design that attracted one of the largest samples of any psychologically-oriented Internet-based study to date. We had varying success rates with 12 different methods of recruiting participants, especially for reaching our target audience. We hope other researchers will consider using the Internet for data collection where possible and continue to develop and refine appropriate methodologies.

REFERENCES

Agocha, V.B., & Cooper, M.L. (1999). Risk perceptions and safer-sex intentions: Does a partner's physical attractiveness undermine the use of risk-relevant information? *Personality and Social Psychology Bulletin, 25,* 746-759.

Anderson, S., & Gansneder, B. (1995). Using electronic mail surveys and computer monitored data for studying computer-mediated communication systems. *Social Science Computer Review, 13 (1),* 33-45.

Buchanan, T., & Smith, J. (1999). Research on the Internet: Validation of a World-Wide Web mediated personality scale. *Behavior Research Methods, Instruments, & Computers, 31 (4),* 565-571.

Davis, R. (1999). Web-based administration of a personality questionnaire: Comparison with traditional methods. *Behavior Research Methods, Instruments, & Computers, 31 (4),* 572-577.

Epstein, J., & Klinkenberg, W.D. (2000). From Eliza to Internet. Unpublished manuscript.

Kaye, B., & Johnson, T. (1999). Research methodology: Taming the cyber frontier. *Social Science Computer Review, 17 (3),* 323-337.

Klinkenberg, W.D., Epstein, J., Scandell, D., & Faulkner, K. (2000). Replication of traditionally collected data via Internet methodology: Determinants of gay and lesbian safer sex practices. Unpublished Manuscript.

Michalak, E. (1998). The use of the Internet as a research tool: The nature and characteristics of seasonal affective disorder (SAD) amongst a population of users. *Interacting with Computers, 9,* 349-365.

Nicholson, T., White, J., & Duncan, D. (1998). Drugnet: A pilot study of adult recreational drug use via the WWW. *Substance Abuse, 19 (3),* 109-120.

Pasveer, K., & Ellard, J. (1998). The making of a personality inventory: Help from the WWW. *Behavior Research Methods, Instruments, & Computers, 30 (2),* 309-313.

Pettit, F. (1999). Exploring the use of the World Wide Web as a psychology data collection tool. *Computers in Human Behavior, 15,* 67-71.

Richard, D. (2000). Assessing posttraumatic stress symptoms in an international sample via the World Wide Web. Unpublished Manuscript.

Stones, A., & Perry, D. (1997). Survey questionnaire data on panic attacks gathered using the World Wide Web. *Depression and Anxiety, 6,* 86-87.

Swoboda, W., Muhlberger, N., Weitkunat, R., & Schneeweiss, S. (1997). Internet surveys by direct mailing. *Social Science Computer Review, 15 (3),* 242-255.

Welch, N., & Krantz, J. (1996). The world-wide-web as a medium for psychoacoustical demonstrations and experiments: Experience and results. *Behavior Research Methods, Instruments, & Computers, 28,* 192-196.

Methodological and Ethical Challenges of Researching a Computer-Mediated Group

Sharon S. Kleinman

SUMMARY. People are increasingly using e-mail technology to join computer-mediated groups, and these groups are gaining the attention of researchers from diverse fields. Researchers are adapting techniques used to study "traditional" contexts, such as face-to-face groups, and devising strategies for meeting the methodological and ethical challenges of studying online interactions. Because studying computer-mediated groups is still a relatively new endeavor, research standards have not yet been codified. Some researchers of computer-mediated groups seem to be unreflexive about the fact that there are real people behind the computer screens who can be affected by the research process–positively or negatively. This paper closely examines one study of a computer-mediated group that used multiple methods, discusses the rationale for decisions made about the research design and procedures, and provides suggestions for scholars interested in studying computer-mediated groups. *[Article copies available for a fee from The Haworth Document Delivery Service: 1-800-HAWORTH. E-mail address: <getinfo@haworthpressinc.com> Website: <http://www.HaworthPress.com> © 2002 by The Haworth Press, Inc. All rights reserved.]*

Sharon S. Kleinman (PhD, Cornell 1998) is Assistant Professor of Communication at Quinnipiac University. Her research interests are at the crossroads of communication, science, and technology.

The author thanks Julian Kilker, Bertram Bradley, and the anonymous reviewers for helpful suggestions.

Address correspondence to the author at Department of Mass Communications, Quinnipiac University, 275 Mount Carmel Avenue, Hamden, CT 06518 (E-mail: Sharon.kleinman@mciworld.com).

[Haworth co-indexing entry note]: "Methodological and Ethical Challenges of Researching a Computer-Mediated Group." Kleinman, Sharon S. Co-published simultaneously in *Journal of Technology in Human Services* (The Haworth Press, Inc.) Vol. 19, No. 2/3, 2002, pp. 49-63; and: *Using the Internet as a Research Tool for Social Work and Human Services* (ed: Goutham M. Menon) The Haworth Press, Inc., 2002, pp. 49-63. Single or multiple copies of this article are available for a fee from The Haworth Document Delivery Service [1-800-HAWORTH, 9:00 a.m. - 5:00 p.m. (EST). E-mail address: getinfo@haworthpressinc.com].

KEYWORDS. Computer-mediated communication, research methods, online social research

INTRODUCTION

People are increasingly using e-mail to participate in computer-mediated groups (Parks & Floyd, 1997). These groups–ranging from soap opera fan clubs (Baym, 1997) to professionally-oriented support groups for women in science and engineering (Kleinman, 1998) to health-oriented support groups for people with disabilities (Braithwaite, Waldron, & Finn, 1999) and diseases (Scheerhorn, Warisse, & McNeilis, 1995)–are gaining researchers' attention because of the diverse and evolving activities that are taking place in them. Researchers from a variety of disciplines, including communication, anthropology, sociology, psychology, linguistics, and science and technology studies, are now facing the challenges of devising reliable and valid methods for studying interactions in computer-mediated contexts that differ from face-to-face on several dimensions that have important implications for the research process: the physical environment, time and space constraints, and modes of communication supported (both one-to-many and one-to-one). This paper explores the methodological and ethical challenges of researching a computer-mediated group using a case study approach. The research process of a four-year study of a computer-mediated group is reviewed, rationales for methodological choices made are discussed, and suggestions are provided for researchers interested in studying computer-mediated groups.

CASE STUDY OF OURNET RESEARCH PROJECT

The research context for the study was OURNET (a pseudonym), an online mailing list (listserv) with approximately 800 members who discussed issues of interest to women in science and engineering. The study explored how some women in these fields are using computer-mediated groups as resources for social support, information, role models, and mentors (Kleinman, 1998). An online mailing list is an asynchronous one-to-many communication system. People who subscribe to the list receive all messages posted to it. OURNET was unmoderated and had no membership restrictions.

Of the many research approaches possible, conducting a case study of OURNET that combined several methods was most appropriate because I was interested in exploring the benefits that this computer-mediated group provided its members, rather than in testing hypotheses about computer-mediated groups or computer-mediated communication. In other words, I was interested in studying "contextual conditions," as the following research questions from the study illustrate (Yin, 1994, p. 13):[1]

1. What are people's reasons for joining an online discussion that identifies a marginalized group?
2. What are the perceived benefits of participating in an online discussion for members of a marginalized group?
3. How does people's level of identification with an online discussion group relate to their level of public participation?
4. What is the nature of the postings to an online discussion that identifies a marginalized group? (Kleinman, 1998, p. 28)

When I designed the OURNET study, I considered issues raised in a series of articles about online social research that appeared in a special issue of *The Information Society* (King, 1996; Reid, 1996), ideas presented in an article comparing the development of online social research to the development of anthropology (Kilker & Kleinman, 1997), guidelines proposed in Schrum's (1995) article about ethical research in the information age, as well as discussions about the research process outlined in texts that focus on social research in "traditional" contexts (Allport, 1942; Babbie, 1995; Fetterman, 1998; Krippendorff, 1980; Reinharz, 1992; Yin, 1994).

Three methods were used in the OURNET study–online participant observation, interviewing, and content analysis. Methodological issues that were addressed included: choosing appropriate data collection methods, obtaining representative samples of participants to interview and e-mail messages to content analyze, developing valid content analysis categories, assessing the reliability of the content analysis coding, and addressing copyright and fair use issues regarding e-mail messages posted to a public listserv.

Ethical issues that were addressed included: gaining access to the research site, obtaining consent from the fluctuating population of participants in the computer-mediated group, engaging participants as co-researchers in the data analysis process, and giving back to participants by making the research findings available to them.

Interviewing Procedures

At the beginning of this study I posted a message to OURNET in which I identified myself as a long-term OURNET member, explained the research project, and asked for permission to study the group and for volunteer interviewees. My e-mail address and home phone number were included in the message so that anybody with questions or concerns could contact me easily. Dozens of people volunteered to be interviewed, and nobody expressed concern about my presence in the group as a researcher.

In-depth, semi-structured interviews were conducted with OURNET members in order to learn about the insiders' perspectives about OURNET. Interviews were conducted over the phone because the interviewees lived all over the world. With the interviewees' permission, the interviews were audiotaped and the recordings were transcribed later.

The pool of interviewees represented the range of participation levels—lurkers, occasional contributors, and frequent contributors. The interviewees' self-reports of participation were compared with the number of messages that they posted during the data collection period and no discrepancies were found. Interviewing lurkers was necessary for investigating their motivation for joining the computer-mediated group and perceived benefits. These topics are particularly interesting from the perspective of lurkers because one of the most commented on aspects of the Internet is its interactivity, even though many more people lurk than participate in online environments (Kiesler, 1997; Rojo & Ragsdale, 1997; Sproull & Faraj, 1997).

Although dozens of people volunteered to be interviewed, 21 interviews were conducted. I stopped interviewing OURNET members when I reached the point of data saturation—when many different people were providing me with the same or similar information. Nineteen of the interviews were with current OURNET members and two were with former members. Interviewing former members allowed me to address the limitations and utility of computer-mediated group membership with people who had left the group for one reason or another.

Content Analysis Procedures

All of the e-mail messages posted to OURNET during a consecutive 125-day period that included one summer month (August) and two fall months (September and October) were archived. These three months were chosen because I anticipated variations in people's participation in OURNET during the summer months because many OURNET members were academics working on a nine-month schedule. In selecting the months for collecting messages, the goal was to ensure that the messages sampled were representative of the larger population from which they were chosen. This was an instance in which having been a long-term participant observer in OURNET provided insights into which months had typical participation levels.

As a systematic examination of the OURNET discussions, content analysis was used to assess how frequently OURNET members addressed various topics, and in which contexts, and to identify patterns and conventions in message postings. These data were triangulated with information that the interviewees reported about the content and purposes of OURNET messages.

Assumptions underlying the content analysis were that the content of the e-mail messages could be categorized inductively and that online discussions evolve over time. The implication of the second assumption was that the e-mail messages should be studied in the context of conversation threads–clusters of messages with interrelated themes. As in Sproull and Faraj's (1997) research of Usenet groups, the unit of analysis was threads composed of seed messages and interrelated responses to these catalyzing messages. The threads were discerned by reviewing the messages in the archive in chronological order.

The archive of OURNET messages was analyzed in chronological order three times. The first review of the messages focused on their manifest content (Babbie, 1995; Krippendorff, 1980) and on demographic information about message senders indicated in their e-mail addresses and signature files. Manifest content refers to what is directly in the text of the messages and contrasts with latent content, which refers to the underlying meaning of the messages. Message categories were discerned inductively. Key informants who had been long-time OURNET members reviewed the categories to check for construct validity.

During the second analysis, messages were coded into categories. In cases in which the content of a message fit more than one category, the message was coded based on the predominant content of the message. The third analysis of the messages focused on discerning the topics of messages and patterns in discussion threads. The entire texts of the messages were analyzed, rather than just the subject header lines, because subject headers do not always reflect message content. In addition, e-mail messages were categorized as *solo* messages to which nobody in the discussion group replied, *seed* messages that catalyzed other messages in response, starting a thread, and *responses* to other messages.

A subset of the archived messages was coded by an independent computer-mediated communication researcher who was given working definitions of the content categories. The independent coder's categorization of the e-mail messages matched my categorization 93% of the time. This was an important step for checking the coding categories and the reliability of the content analysis process.

Conclusion

This study of the computer-mediated group OURNET involved online participant observation, in-depth interviewing of OURNET members, and content analysis of e-mail messages posted to OURNET. Key informants reviewed the content analysis categories to check for construct validity. An independent researcher coded a subset of the e-mail message archive to check the content analysis reliability. Twenty-one interview transcriptions were analyzed. The content analysis and interview data were complementary sources of information about the meanings of OURNET for the participants. Online participant observation over a four-year period informed the interview and content analysis processes.

METHODOLOGICAL AND ETHICAL ISSUES ADDRESSED DURING OURNET STUDY

Ethical issues such as obtaining informed consent from research participants, maintaining their privacy, and protecting them from harm, can be slippery in research about computer-mediated groups because research standards for studying these groups have not yet been codified and because of the relative ease of data collection (Kilker & Kleinman, 1997; King, 1996).

The first methodological and ethical issue that every researcher must address involves gaining access to the research site. Because OURNET was a public listserv with no membership requirements, gaining access was not difficult; I subscribed to the list by sending an e-mail message to a computer that automatically added my e-mail address to the list of addresses that received all OURNET messages.

I had been an OURNET member as an informal participant observer for three years before I commenced this project. However, once I began this project, I needed to obtain informed consent from OURNET participants to study their interactions and the content of their postings.

Gaining informed consent from all participants in an ongoing computer-mediated group can be a challenge because these groups have fluctuating populations; new members, including researchers, can join a public group without the group's knowledge or consent. (This would not be the case in computer-mediated groups with restricted membership, such as Systers, a group for women in computer science that Winter and Huff [1996] studied.)

Data concerning computer-mediated groups can be collected relatively easily: A computer can be used unobtrusively as a "research assistant" to collect, archive, and even analyze e-mail messages without the group's knowledge or consent (Fetterman, 1998; Kilker & Kleinman, 1997). Unlike a sociologist studying a neighborhood, researchers studying a computer-mediated group might never meet face-to-face with the members of the computer-mediated group they are studying, because the group members could be spread all over the world. Thus, even in cases in which the data collection process is interactive, involving telephone or e-mail interviews for example, researchers can forget on some level that they are dealing with real people.

One study of a computer-mediated group for sexual abuse survivors (Finn & Lavitt, 1994) exemplifies researchers' insufficient attention to ethical issues concerning informed consent, confidentiality, and privacy reminiscent of Humphrey's (1970) infamous *Tearoom trade* study: Finn and Lavitt

> downloaded, analyzed, and published notes, making no request to the individuals of the group for permission. This occurred even though Finn reported the existence of a note from the moderator of the group saying that interested professionals who were not sexual abuse survivors were discouraged from joining the group. The exact dates and times that sample notes were posted, as well as the name of the group, appear in the published results. Finn states that since "messages posted on a BBS (bulletin board system) are public information," changing the names on the sample messages they reprinted would insure the privacy of the BBS users. (King, 1996, p. 122)[2]

While using pseudonyms would protect the anonymity of the individual message posters, the researchers' actions in this case could have destroyed group members' perception of the group as being a safe and private space for discussing personal issues (King, 1996). Because published reports could have had deleterious effects on the functionality of the group, it seems obvious that these researchers did not take adequate precautions to protect the people studied from harm.

Issues of informed consent, confidentiality, and privacy can be further complicated when a researcher is studying the archived e-mail messages of a computer-mediated group that no longer exists.[3] It is still incumbent on the researcher to protect the confidentiality and privacy of those who wrote the e-mail messages if the study deals with a controversial topic or if reports about the research could negatively affect those who were studied.

To address the issue of informed consent in the OURNET study, I posted a message to the group explaining the project and encouraging anyone with questions or concerns about it to contact me. In this message I also asked for volunteers to be interviewed about their experiences in the group. Dozens of people volunteered, and nobody expressed concern about my presence in the group as a researcher. It is possible that the fact that I mentioned in my e-mail message that I was a long-time OURNET member helped the participants to feel comfortable with my project. Nevertheless, someone who joined OURNET after I posted the message might have had concerns had they known about the project. I decided to take this risk because I thought that a daily message about the project requesting consent from new members would have been disruptive. Announcing the study again at the conclusion of the research period to see if any members who were new since my initial posting objected to the research would have strengthened my informed consent.[4]

Maintaining OURNET members' confidentiality and privacy was important because members often discussed controversial issues and revealed personal information in their messages to OURNET. As a first step toward protecting OURNET members' confidentiality and privacy, I used a pseudonym for the group (OURNET) and pseudonyms for all participants. In addition, all identifying information was stripped from excerpts of interview transcriptions and e-mail messages in reports about the project. However, an interested (and motivated) person might be able to discover the real name of the group and could then access the publicly-available archive of OURNET messages, and perform keyword searches using quotes from e-mail messages, that were reprinted in research reports. At that point, it might be possible for the "researcher" to identify the sender of a message and the sender's institutional affiliation based on signature files at the end of the message or the e-mail address from which the message originated. As I selected excerpts to reprint in reports, I was mindful of this potential breach of

OURNET members' confidentiality and privacy and therefore refrained from reprinting some quotes (cf. Reid, 1996).

Addressing Issues of Copyright and Fair Use

Another methodological issue in this project involved the copyright ownership of e-mail messages posted to OURNET.

> Under the Copyright Act of 1976 (title 17 of the *United States Code*) an unpublished work is copyrighted from the moment it is fixed in tangible form–for example, typed on a page. . . . Until the author formally transfers copyright . . . the author owns the copyright on an unpublished manuscript, and all exclusive rights due the owner of the copyright are also due the owner of an unpublished work. (American Psychological Association, 1994, p. 299)

The "tangible form" does not have to be permanent, but the "medium must be sufficiently permanent or stable to allow it to be perceived, copied or otherwise communicated for more than a transitory duration" (Moore, 1999, p. 501). This means that the author of an e-mail message owns the copyright, unless the author transfers it, or the e-mail message was a work made for hire, or the e-mail message was prepared by an employee within the scope of her job. There are other exceptions to copyright ownership that might apply to some e-mail messages, including works in the public domain, such as U. S. Government works, or works on which copyright has expired.

Educators and students should exercise caution when downloading materials from the Internet for use in scholarly or instructional works

> because there is a mix of works protected by copyright and works in the public domain on the network. Access to works on the Internet does not automatically mean that these can be reproduced and reused without permission or royalty payment and, furthermore, some copyrighted works may have been posted to the Internet without authorization of the copyright holder. (Moore, 1999, p. 631)

Although only a court of law can authoritatively determine on a case-by-case basis whether a particular use of copyrighted material is a fair use or not, there are guidelines concerning the fair use of copyrighted materials:

Section 107 of the Copyright Act sets forth the four use factors which should be considered in each instance, based on the particular facts of a given case, to determine whether a use is a "fair use": (1) the purpose and character of use, including whether such use is of a commercial nature or is for nonprofit educational purposes, (2) the nature of the copyrighted work, (3) the amount and substantiality of the portion used in relation to the copyrighted work as a whole, and (4) the effect of the use upon the potential market for or value of the copyrighted work. (Moore, 1999, p. 626)

This section of the Copyright Act provides "examples of purposes that can involve fair use of copyrighted material, including criticism, comment, news reporting, teaching (including multiple copies for classroom use), scholarship, or research" (Moore, 1999, p. 524). Considering these stipulations, it seems likely that a court would consider judicious quoting of e-mail messages that had been posted to a public computer-mediated group for use in academic articles to be a fair use.

Determining Population Demographics

Determining the population demographics of a computer-mediated group can be challenging. For one thing, people can add or remove themselves from a computer-mediated group easily and often invisibly. The list owner or moderator might be willing to provide the researcher with a copy of the membership roster. This roster will be a snapshot of the population at one point in time. In the OURNET study, I e-mailed my request to the list administrator, and she told me which commands to use to download a publicly-available membership roster that included members' e-mail addresses and names. Cross-referencing this information with information contained in archived e-mail messages enabled me to discern the sex distribution of OURNET members as well as their institutional affiliations (e.g., colleges, military, government), and to some extent their geographic locations.

To determine the sex distribution of OURNET members, the membership roster was examined. This process involved taking most names at face value as being typically masculine or feminine. However, some names are androgynous, some people use only their initials, and some people use nicknames. In addition, some groups allow members to suppress their names and e-mail addresses from publicly-available rosters. All of these permutations can make it difficult for a researcher to determine the sex distribution of the population in a computer-mediated group or the sex of an individual member, without asking members directly (on a questionnaire, for example) or triangulating with other data. In addition, it can be difficult to judge the sex of a person in a computer-mediated group based on a name if the name is foreign. Again, data triangulation–which might include reading messages the person posted to the group–can often solve this problem. I determined that one OURNET member who had an Asian name was a woman when I read one of her postings about an experience that her husband had at work.

Obtaining Representative Samples

Obtaining representative samples of participants to interview and e-mail messages to content analyze were additional challenges in the data collection process of the OURNET study. Although in a qualitative, exploratory study it is not necessary to interview a random sample, it is still important to interview a representative sample. To address the issue of selection bias resulting from having volunteer interviewees, several interviewees were recruited based on the recommendations of others in the group. For the purposes of my study, it was important to interview members with diverse institutional affiliations, varied job statuses (professors, graduate students, and scientists working in industry, for example) as well as diverse levels of participation in the group (lurkers and non-lurkers). To insure that the interviewees were representative of the computer-mediated group in terms of participation levels, the interviewees' self-reports of their OURNET participation were compared to their actual levels of participation, which was determined by examining the message archive. To insure that the interviewees represented the diversity of institutional affiliations and job statuses, they were asked a series of demographic questions.

Involving Group Members as Co-Analysts and Giving Back to the Group

Engaging OURNET members as co-analysts was important for checking construct validity (Yin, 1994). Key informants reviewed the content analysis categories and drafts of research reports. These informants helped refine content analysis categories, enhance interpretations of the diverse meanings and benefits of OURNET membership, and ultimately improve reports about the findings of the study.

At the end of the study, I made a report summarizing the findings available to OURNET members as a way of giving back to the group that had generously shared their experiences and insights and had allowed me to examine their online interactions. (See Reinharz, 1992 for discussions of reciprocity in feminist social research that informed the OURNET study.)

DISCUSSION

This examination of the OURNET study illustrated two main points in particular: the importance of methodological and data triangulation in online social research for fostering a comprehensive analysis, and the necessity of taking extra precautions to insure that online social research is conducted in an ethical manner.

In the OURNET study, I found that long-term participant observation provided the opportunity for me to become familiar with OURNET's members and history (cf. Baym, 1997; Cherny, 1995). This familiarity enabled me to discuss past conversation threads and controversies in an informed manner with interviewees. The in-depth interviews provided an opportunity for me to explore members' experiences in and perspectives about OURNET in a depth and with a sensitivity that other research approaches, such as surveys, would not necessarily allow. As a complement to the interviews, content analysis provided a systematic examination of members' participation patterns and the content of the messages.

Interview and content analysis data were iteratively analyzed and triangulated. Methodological and data triangulation were critical because any one research or data collection method developed for studying other communication contexts is likely to be inadequate for online contexts, especially at this relatively early stage of online research (Kilker & Kleinman, 1997). This is the case for a variety of reasons, including that interactions in online contexts have reduced and different social cues, and communicators have reduced social presence vis-à-vis other communication contexts, such as face-to-face (Sproull & Kiesler, 1991; Walther, 1992; also cf. Short, Williams, & Christie, 1976). Moreover, people who join computer-mediated groups have different levels of computer competence and "computer reticence" (Turkle, 1984, 1988). Just as people are variably comfortable in face-to-face contexts, in online environments people are variably comfortable both socially and technically, and their comfort level affects what they say, and even if they say anything at all. Data collection and analysis techniques need to take into account people's different levels of comfort and competence online.

The OURNET study also highlighted another quality of computer-mediated communication that should be factored into research designs: computer-mediated communication can be public or private (one-to-many or one-to-one). Public e-mail messages sent to a computer-mediated group might only be a fraction of the interactions among group members because members use private e-mail when a topic is sensitive or controversial, when they want to disclose personal information, when their goals differ from the group's goals, or when they eschew public posting for other reasons, such as privacy concerns or fear of flaming. Private e-mail conversations took place among members of OURNET–they were alluded to in public postings to the group. Interviewing members allowed me to find out about these types of interactions.

In sum, studying computer-mediated groups is still a relatively new endeavor, and the implications of this work as well as researchers' ethical responsibilities are not always clear. This paper reviewed in detail one study of a computer-mediated group that used multiple methods, discussed the rationale for decisions made about the research design and procedures, highlighted sticky points in the research process, and provided suggestions for scholars interested in studying computer-mediated groups. As computer-mediated groups continue to evolve in ways we haven't yet imagined, researchers will undoubtedly face new methodological and ethical issues that will challenge us to again refine our methods and clarify our ethical responsibilities.

NOTES

1. See Yin (1994) for a comprehensive description and rationale for the case study approach.

2. Like King (1996), I apologize to the members of the group Finn and Lavitt (1994) studied for the additional publicity. Five years after Finn and Lavitt's article was published and three years after King's, researchers have continued to use the actual names of computer-mediated groups they have studied.

3. "Archived e-mail and Usenet records represent an increasingly accepted source of data for research, but these materials are becoming inaccessible as the technology to read old computer formats disappears and the computer tapes themselves decay," as Kilker (1999, p. 263) found in examining a group from the 1970's.

4. I thank an anonymous reviewer for this suggestion.

REFERENCES

Allport, G. (1942). *The use of personal documents in psychological science.* New York: Social Science Research Council.

American Psychological Association. (1994). *Publication manual of the American Psychological Association* (4th ed.). Washington, DC: American Psychological Association.

Babbie, E. (1995). *The practice of social research* (7th ed.). New York: Wadsworth Publishing Company.

Baym, N. K. (1997). Interpreting soap operas and creating community: Inside an electronic fan culture. In S. Kiesler (Ed.), *Culture of the internet* (pp. 103-120). Mahwah, NJ: Lawrence Erlbaum Associates.

Braithwaite, D. O., Waldron, V. R., & Finn, J. (1999). Communication of social support in computer-mediated groups for people with disabilities. *Health Communication, 11* (2), 123-151.

Cherny, L. (1995). *The MUD register: Conversational modes of action in a text-based virtual reality.* Unpublished doctoral dissertation, Stanford University.

Fetterman, D. M. (1998). *Ethnography: Step by step* (2nd ed.). Thousand Oaks, CA: Sage.

Finn, J., & Lavitt, M. (1994). Computer based self-help groups for sexual abuse survivors. *Social Work with Groups, 17,* 21-46.

Humphreys, R. A. L. (1970). *Tearoom trade: Sex in public places.* Chicago, IL: Aldine.

Kiesler, S. (1997). *Culture of the internet.* Mahwah, NJ: Lawrence Erlbaum Associates.

Kilker, J. A. (1999). *Networking identity: A case study examining social interactions and identity in the early development of e-mail technology.* Unpublished doctoral dissertation, Cornell University.

Kilker, J. A., & Kleinman, S. S. (1997). Researching online environments: Lessons from the history of anthropology. *The New Jersey Journal of Communication, 5* (1), 66-83.

King, S. A. (1996). Researching Internet communities: Proposed ethical guidelines for the reporting of results. *The Information Society, 12,* 119-127.

Kleinman, S. S. (1998). *Membership has its benefits: Computer-mediated communication and social identification in an online discussion group for women in science and engineering.* Unpublished doctoral dissertation, Cornell University.

Krippendorff, K. (1980). *Content analysis: An introduction to its methodology.* Newbury Park, CA: Sage.

Moore, R. L. (1999). *Mass communication law and ethics* (2nd ed.). Mahwah, NJ: Lawrence Erlbaum Associates.

Parks, M. R., & Floyd, K. (1997). Making friends in cyberspace. *Journal of Communication, 46* (1), 80-97.

Reid, E. (1996). Informed consent in the study of on-line communities: A reflection on the effects of computer-mediated social research. *The Information Society, 12,* 169-174.

Reinharz, S. (1992). *Feminist methods in social research*. New York: Oxford University Press.

Rojo, A., & Ragsdale, R. G. (1997). A process perspective on participation in scholarly electronic forums. *Science Communication, 18* (4), 320-341.

Scheerhorn, D., Warisse, J., & McNeilis, K. S. (1995). Computer-based telecommunication among an illness-related community: Design, delivery, early use, and the functions of HIGHnet. *Health Communication, 7* (4), 301-325.

Schrum, L. (1995). Framing the debate: Ethical research in the information age. *Qualitative Inquiry, 1* (3), 311-326.

Short, J., Williams, E., & Christie, B. (1976). *The social psychology of telecommunications*. Chichester: John Wiley.

Sproull, L., & Faraj, S. (1997). Atheism, sex, and databases: The net as a social technology. In S. Kiesler (Ed.), *Culture of the internet* (pp. 35-51). Mahwah, NJ: Lawrence Erlbaum Associates.

Sproull, L., & Kiesler, S. (1991). *Connections*. Cambridge, MA: The MIT Press.

Turkle, S. (1984). *The second self: Computers and the human spirit*. New York: Touchstone.

Turkle, S. (1988). Computational reticence: Why women fear the intimate machine. In C. Kramarae (Ed.), *Technology and women's voices: Keeping in touch* (pp. 41-61). London, UK: Routledge.

Walther, J. B. (1992). Interpersonal effects in computer-mediated interaction. *Communication Research, 19* (1), 52-90.

Winter, D., & Huff, C. (1996). Adapting the Internet: Comments from a women-only electronic forum. *American Sociologist, 27* (1), 30-54.

Yin, R. K. (1994). *Case study research: Design and methods* (2nd ed.). Thousand Oaks, CA: Sage.

Prospects and Limitations
of Psychological Testing on the Internet

Azy Barak

Nicole English

SUMMARY. Internet-based psychological testing is a recent extension of computerized testing, a technology developed in the 1980s. The new procedure possesses the benefits and costs of computerized testing and introduces several new fascinating professional opportunities as well as new problems. Side by side with professional tests, numerous, mostly unmoderated, popular, quasi-psychological tests have been published on the Internet in different diagnostic areas: intelligence and special aptitudes, personality traits, emotional states, attitudes and attitude sets, interpersonal and social behavior dispositions, vocational interests and preferences, and more. Net surfers may take most tests for free and receive immediate feedback. Although there are great benefits to this new procedure, risks and problems exist, too. This article reviews representative Internet-based psychological tests and discusses their professional status. Cumulative research that tries to shed light on the possible utility of this testing procedure is surveyed. The prospects and advantages as well as the problems and limitations are discussed, as are proposals aimed at maximizing the former and minimizing the latter. A plea for in-

Azy Barak is affiliated with the Department of Psychology, University of Haifa, Israel.

Nicole English is affiliated with the Computer Science Department, University of Missouri, 5100 Rockhill Road, Kansas City, MO 64110 (E-mail: nenglish@CSTP. EDU).

Address correspondence to: Azy Barak, Department of Psychology, University of Haifa, Mount Carmel, Haifa 31905, Israel (E-mail: azy@construct.haifa.ac.il).

[Haworth co-indexing entry note]: "Prospects and Limitations of Psychological Testing on the Internet." Barak, Azy, and Nicole English. Co-published simultaneously in *Journal of Technology in Human Services* (The Haworth Press, Inc.) Vol. 19, No. 2/3, 2002, pp. 65-89; and: *Using the Internet as a Research Tool for Social Work and Human Services* (ed: Goutham M. Menon) The Haworth Press, Inc., 2002, pp. 65-89. Single or multiple copies of this article are available for a fee from The Haworth Document Delivery Service [1-800-HAWORTH, 9:00 a.m. - 5:00 p.m. (EST). E-mail address: getinfo@haworthpressinc.com].

65

tensive research, as well as additional and different types of measures, is voiced. *[Article copies available for a fee from The Haworth Document Delivery Service: 1-800-HAWORTH. E-mail address: <getinfo@haworthpressinc.com> Website: <http://www.HaworthPress.com> © 2002 by The Haworth Press, Inc. All rights reserved.]*

KEYWORDS. Testing, assessment, online, Internet, World Wide Web

The use of personal computers for psychological testing is not a new procedure. Although it is not entirely clear when the first attempt was made in this direction, publications on the procedure emerged almost two decades ago (Byers, 1981). With the development and sophistication of computer and communications technology and the training of professional users, computerized testing has become widespread. Personal computers–either as independent machines or as part of a local network–have been used successfully for testing purposes in organizations (Zickar, Overton, Taylor, & Harms, 1999), counseling and clinical agencies (Sampson, 1990), and schools (Kingsbury & Houser, 1999). Cumulative research clearly shows that computerized tests maintain the measurement reliability and validity of the original paper-and-pencil tests in different testing domains (Campbell et al., 1999; DiLalla, 1996; Neuman & Baydoun, 1998). In recent years, however, the introduction to psychology and the mental health professions of Internet communication and of advanced Internet technologies and software (Barak, 1999) has offered a new means of delivering psychological tests. This opportunity, in fact, has been exploited by many individuals and agencies alike through a great number of websites offering numerous psychological tests and questionnaires for diverse purposes: from mere entertainment to professional diagnostics to research data collection. The purposes of the current article are as follows: (a) to describe and discuss psychological testing procedures on the Internet; (b) to consider the pros and cons of Internet-based psychological testing; (c) to review the current available research on Internet-based psychological tests; (d) to discuss relevant legal and ethical issues; and (e) to propose directions for future research and development on this subject.

COMPUTERIZED TESTING:
POTENTIAL BENEFITS AND PROBABLE COSTS

Internet-based testing includes all the advantages and disadvantages of personal (micro) computer-based testing, but introduces additional factors, negative and positive. Therefore, a brief review of computerized psychological testing should precede the discussion and evaluation of Internet-based testing.

Two basic procedures exist for computerized testing: (a) simple conversion of paper-and-pencil tests into computerized form and (b) more advanced computerized adaptive testing. In the former case, test items and instructions are simply typed into a computer program. The program presents the instructions and trial or sample items to test-takers on a computer screen; respondents mark their responses through (usually) mouse clicks. Test-takers may move forward or backward along the items, change answers, and do anything they would have done on an equivalent paper-and-pencil test. The computer program also monitors the testing time of time-limited tests, and it may present additional tests if a test battery is used. Upon completion of the administration of the test, the program computes raw and standardized scores according to pre-programmed instructions. The usual options available are the following: supplying on-screen and/or printed test results to test-takers, providing test-takers with an overall evaluation, accumulating data to update test norms, and saving data for research purposes. In using the second procedure, Item Response Theory (see a recent review by Harvey & Hammer, 1999) is adopted to create adaptive testing. In this case, test-takers may respond, not to *all* test items, but to a minimum number of individually determined items that best predict the final test score/s. The number and nature of the items to be included in the test are either computer-determined (i.e., computerized adaptive testing) or self-determined (i.e., self-adaptive testing). In this procedure, the computer has the obvious advantage of mathematically estimating (according to a preset algorithm) optimal item collection to provide the most valid test scores (see Meijer & Nering, 1999).

Computerized tests present several clear advantages over standardized paper-and-pencil tests. First, disposable materials are saved. This advantage has implications for both short and long-range costs, for convenience of test administration, and for environmental protection. Second, because the tests are fully automated, they are more standardized in terms of test instructions and time-keeping. Third, precise scores can be calculated very rapidly, with unfortunate common human mistakes obviated and much time saved, especially in complicated-to-score tests and inventories. Fourth, scores may be automatically and easily added to a test's database to adjust norms and to be used for research. This advantage, too, may save considerable expense in terms of labor costs. In addition, the very availability of data sets may encourage research.

Fifth, test-takers have the advantage (in case this option is provided) of receiving immediate, objective, expert-based narrative feedback of their test findings. Moreover, if a complicated inventory or test battery is administered, a comprehensive, automated evaluation may be provided instantly, as well.

Alongside these advantages, there are several disadvantages and limitations to computerized tests. First, for test administrators, this procedure necessitates at least a basic knowledge in computer operations and sometimes also in programming. Although the need for computer literacy seems to be obvious in recent years, this may be a limiting factor for older professionals. Second, for test-takers, there are indications that computer skills—at least typing speed—may be related to test achievement (Russell, 1999). It should be noted, however, that this factor was found to be related to performance in open-ended tests, not multiple-choice tests (Russell & Haney, 1997). Third, there is debate about the accuracy of the computer interpretation of test scores, a problem that may become paramount in cases when comprehensive test batteries, or series of tests, are administered. Fourth, computerized tests might be inappropriate for test-takers who suffer from computer anxiety, as a unique, irrelevant error-variance might be introduced into observed scores, thus impairing test-result validity. This point has also been mentioned in relation to gender differences, the argument being that women, because of their greater computer anxiety and less computer sophistication, benefit less than men from computerized testing (Lankford, Bell, & Elias, 1994). This argument, however, has yielded inconsistent empirical findings (Anderson, 1996; Chua, Chen, & Wong, 1999; Miles & King, 1998). Similarly, in regard to age differences (i.e., older people are more computer anxious, hence are at a disadvantage with computerized tests); these have become minimal, as well (Dyck, Gee, & Smither, 1999).

Although not yet widespread, computerized psychological tests are flourishing. Many psychological tests have both paper-and-pencil and computer versions, the type selected by test administrators and/or takers according to specific local considerations.

FROM PERSONAL COMPUTER TO INTERNET-BASED PSYCHOLOGICAL TESTING

The formation of the Internet and its exploitation by psychology (Barak, 1999; Sampson, Kolodinsky, & Greeno, 1997) created an unprecedented opportunity that has enabled the general public to use various psychological tools and services from a remote system. In the context of testing, the Internet was first exploited to transfer test results quickly and even to deliver complicated psychodiagnostic information for immediate consultation by means of videoconferencing (Ball, Scott, McLaren, & Watson, 1993). More sophisticated, efficient use of the Net for psychological testing soon followed; a test could be uploaded into a server anywhere on the Net, and users could take it from a distance in a place and at a time of their choice. Moreover, the development of CGI scripts and Java applets introduced a wide range of testing possibilities from a distance. Early Internet-based tests and questionnaires were in a form that included only a list of items and scoring instructions; this procedure then changed to computerized scoring, sometimes accompanied by interpretations and recommendations. Although this procedure best fits a multiple-choice testing format and Likert-type questionnaire items, the use of fast Internet communication (i.e., e-mail) made open-ended, even essay format possible, as well.

Internet-based testing requires a remote access connection (such as a phone line) and standard Internet-browsing software. In contrast to personal computer (or local network)-based testing, Internet-based testing does not require test software; the software is installed on a remote server that uses a few, rather standard capabilities of a user's personal computer (e.g., a Web browser, Java-language software, multimedia devices). Access to a particular Internet-based test may be open to all or limited to selected users by means of a password or other mechanism. Test time can be predetermined (by use of Java), but most Internet-based psychological tests are practically unrestricted in terms of time. For most tests, users are instructed to click their responses on an HTML form and to submit it when done through the click of a "send" button. Results, in most cases, are provided in seconds. Internet-based psychological tests include tests of various types and foci: tests of intelligence and of specific scholastic abilities, perceptual tests, clerical tests, measures of a wide range of attitudes, personality inventories and specific personality traits, vocational interests and attitudes, and more. While some of the tests reflect a Web version of preexisting pencil-and-paper tests, others are original.

EXAMPLES OF INTERNET-BASED PSYCHOLOGICAL TESTS

Listed as follows are some representative examples of Internet-based psychological tests to illustrate what is being developed and what is currently available on the Web. These examples are not meant to be an exhaustive list, for there are literally scores from which to choose, and many are quite professional. The examples are intended to be representative, reflecting the variety of types of tests available on the Net. All of the psychological tests discussed here are interactive, Web-browser-based tests that give the test-taker immediate feedback on results.

Psychiatry Information for the General Public, hosted by the New York University Department of Psychiatry (at http://www.med. nyu.edu/ Psych/public.html) offers screening tests for the public related to depression, anxiety, sexual disorders, attention deficit disorder (ADDC), and personality disorders. The website also includes quality informational references on many psychological disorders and links to relevant reading materials. All of the tests are 10-item inventories of symptoms, with 4- or 5-point Likert scales or checklists. All have a disclaimer on the test page and on the results page as well as links for referrals and more information about the condition being tested. For example, Online Screening for Anxiety (OSA) is a 10-item checklist of anxiety-related symptoms. It has a short disclaimer that states, "OSA is a preliminary screening test for anxiety symptoms that does not replace in any way a formal psychiatric evaluation. It is designed to give a preliminary idea about the presence of mild to moderate anxiety symptoms that indicate the need for an evaluation by a psychiatrist." Hitting the submit/results button leads to a Web page with a summary of the symptoms that were checked and a message, "The above answer(s) are anxiety symptoms that might be part of an Anxiety Disorder. It is advised to seek a psychiatric consultation," and links to referral information and information on anxiety from NIMH. The format is similar for the other tests. No psychometric information is provided.

Queendom.com: Tests, tests, tests is a battery of original psychological tests (at http://www.queendom.com/tests.html) offered at no charge to the public. This site is geared toward self-help and personal growth. It includes a short description of what each instrument is intended to measure, clear instructions on how to take the test, and the amount of time each requires. The site offers inventories on anxiety, social anxiety, self-esteem, communication skills, coping skills, assertiveness, Type A personality, lifestyle, extraversion/introversion, sales personality, IQ, jealousy, relationship satisfaction, depression, emotional IQ, leadership, locus of control, burnout, optimism, relationship attachment, PMS, and arguing style. A disclaimer is clearly stated on the homepage: "While psychological tests may help you get to know yourself better, they cannot solve your problems and do not replace professional care."

Each test has a different format, whether Likert scales, multiple choice, checklists, or a combination of these techniques. Scoring is immediate, the results giving feedback on the number of responses, percentages, and percentiles. The Optimism test, for example, provides clear instructions on how to answer the questions, what will happen in the case of an omitted response, and the amount of time it takes to complete. The test has 18 multiple-choice questions and takes 10-20 minutes to complete. Once submitted, the results are reported immediately, giving the range of scores (0-100) and a short narrative of the results. The "Results" page also presents a link to yet another personality test. The site includes referrals to counselors and links to further psychological information. Although there are a number of advertising banners on each page, the layout of the site has a crisp, clean appearance, and it is easy to maneuver. Reliability and validity data are available for most scales. Copyright restrictions are clearly stated with exceptions made for non-commercial research for which the researcher registers to use. With the exception of licensing for research, scoring must be done online with the forms supplied by the website.

Self Discovery Workshop (at http://www.iqtest.com/index.html) is an IQ test provided to the public for free with the hope that takers of the test will purchase the site owners' Complete Personal Intelligence Profile. According to the history of the test, it was developed for the Institute for Self Improvement with the main goal of creating an accurate, quick, and entertaining test that could be marketed commercially to the general population. The site discusses the meaning of the IQ score in terms of academic potential; it cautions readers that scores do not guarantee happiness. The free test gives a complete page of instructions, and the opportunity to take three practice questions. During the actual test, 38 true/false questions are presented, to be answered in approximately 13 minutes. Scores are penalized or increased for completion in more or less than 13 minutes. The results, a general IQ score based on an average of 13 different abilities, are returned immediately. The site claims that the test's results are generally within five points of a professional test. A "Frequently Asked Questions" list is available to those who want more detailed information about how the test is evaluated.

Keirsey Character and Temperament Sorter (at http://keirsey.com/index.html) provides two typological-style personality scales, very similar to the Myers-Briggs Temperament Inventory (MBTI) on which they are based. The first test is a 38-item inventory with a combination of multiple-choice, 4-point Likert scales and two-dimensional checklist. The results, returned immediately, give a graphical representation of one's temperament. The temperament descriptions can be read in detail from the site itself or from the author's book. The second test looks more like the original inventory from the book; it is a 70-item, two-dimensional checklist that gives a graphic display of temperament scores. The site is informational and interesting, but it is more of a promotion for the books than it is therapeutic. No psychometric information is provided.

What's Your Emotional Intelligence Quotient? (at http://www.utne.com/azEQ.tmpl) gives an Emotional Intelligence Quotient test based on Daniel Goleman's book. The site offers a 10-item, multiple-choice test, with immediate feedback detailing how each question is scored. It discusses the basics of emotional intelligence and explains where the score falls relative to an average score. No psychometric information is made available.

Organizational Diagnostics Online's Profiler test (at http://od-online.com/webpage/intro.htm) is described at the website as the "first personality test on the Internet that provides comprehensive feedback written by psychologists." It is a 50-item test that includes sections containing a Likert scale, a checklist inventory, and questions concerning one's position in the workplace. Interpretation provided by trained psychologists, offers a unique profile detailing one's strengths and weaknesses. Results are immediate. The Summary Report evaluating one's personality is free; it includes a description of degree of extroversion, agreeableness, thoroughness, openness to experience, and emotionality. For payment, additional information may be provided, such as on career match, work style, and interpersonal relationships. No psychometric information is made public on this website.

ADVANTAGES AND DISADVANTAGES OF INTERNET-BASED PSYCHOLOGICAL TESTING

Advantages

Electronically-created tests are easy to design, create, alter, and distribute (English, 1996). Almost any word processor or editor can be used to design the instrument; once created in a digital format, it can be converted into whatever form is needed for distribution, be it e-mail or Internet (using browser-based software tools). For the purpose of this article, emphasis is given to browser-based Web technology for testing, and it is assumed that e-mail will be used predominantly to distribute the URL of a Web page containing a test.

One of the advantages directly related to research of using browser-based technology is that it can be used locally (on a personal computer) or remotely (via the Web) or in a combination of both, depending on the needs of the researcher and the situation. This flexibility can allow a researcher to take a laptop to a certain site, collect data, and later use a browser interface to upload the data to a single, centralized location where the data can be scored and archived.

Another advantage of using a browser interface for testing is that a researcher can easily solicit participants who are already on the Web to participate in a study and take a test via the Web (English, 1997). In this way, the participants can take the test at their leisure, in the privacy of their own surroundings, at any time during the day or night. Once the software is in place, the researcher can collect data automatically without having to administer the test personally to each participant. Because of the ease of distribution of Internet-based tests, large numbers of potential participants can be contacted (and can respond) in a relatively short amount of time (Buchanan & Smith, 1999). Depending on the nature of the study, a wide variety of types or a single focus group that might otherwise be difficult to locate can be contacted. The flexibility of a browser interface and Web technology allows a test to be distributed widely, with practically no political or geographical border. Yet, this procedure enables the data and scoring to remain in one central location (be it with the researcher, the publisher, or other copyright holder), which is a great advantage when standardizing new instruments.

Another advantage refers to test-takers' feedback. Depending on how the instrument is to be used, informational feedback can be given to the test-taker or more detailed, diagnostic feedback given to a counselor in a remote area for professional screening. The user may merely take the test or upload the responses and receive results without concern for scoring, which can be done automatically.

An additional advantage relates to the sensitive issue of illegal copying of tests. Depending on how an Internet-based test is laid out, it can be made more difficult to print or reproduce than a paper test. Without the ability to score them, however, the test questions are not very useful. A paper test can be taken to the nearest copying machine and reproduced until resources are exhausted. A Web-test program can be written in such a way that its reproduction would be tedious and difficult. For example, questions can be broken up to appear on different pages, making printing a very lengthy process; or creative colors used to make printing more expensive and time-consuming. In any event, if someone is determined to copy a psychological test, it is generally easier, more convenient, and cheaper to obtain a paper copy of the instrument and have it mass produced than it is to print it off the Web.

There are a few other specific advantages that relate to the specifics of test designing. Data can be collected in a relatively secure way to protect privacy and insure confidentiality. The Web test pages can be constructed with mandatory fields to prevent oversights or omissions during testing. Participants can take a Web test anonymously, in private, and at their own pace, which encourages veracity in responses (Anderson, 1987; Turner, Ku, Rogers, Lindberg, Pleck, & Sonenstein, 1998; Wolford & Rosenberg, 1998). Often, participants feel more comfortable revealing sensitive data about themselves to a computer than to a human interviewer (Kobak, Greist, Jefferson, & Katzelnick, 1996; Turner et al., 1998; Wolford & Rosenberg, 1998). If follow-up is desired, an entry can be created for the participant to leave an e-mail address while the researcher can leave a contact e-mail address on the Web test for future questions. Participants who would like to follow the outcome of a particular study can be given a "results" Web page for further information (English, 1996). This simple procedure may encourage researchers to adhere to APA's (1992) Code of Ethics in regard to providing debriefing and making research results available to participants.

In summary, an Internet-based test is convenient to construct, revise, distribute, and standardize, and it offers a researcher the opportunity to gather a great deal of data in a relatively short amount of time. This type of test is also convenient to take, use, score, and receive informational feedback for the user. Despite the many advantages of browser-based Web tests, however, there are, as with any technology, disadvantages as well, including many of the same ones that hold true for paper testing, unless care is taken.

Disadvantages

One of the obvious disadvantages of Web technology is that a certain amount of Web expertise is needed for a researcher, psychologist, or test administrator or programmer they hire. Fortunately, many Internet software tools are now available on the market to allow a novice user to design and create relatively rapidly a prototype of what is needed for an Internet-based test. Once a prototype is created, a person with Internet programming skills (e.g., research assistant) can work with the researcher or other professional to automate the final working version of the Web test. With adequate documentation in the final program, updates and revisions can be made without much difficulty. The need to have someone on the team who must be familiar with Web technology in order to create or maintain a browser-based test or questionnaire might, however, be considered a disadvantage.

A second disadvantage emanates from the previous one: considerable time must be invested in designing, creating, and testing an Internet-based test. Often, the social system or the organizational context in which the test developer is operating supports another medium (such as paper-and-pencil) and may not be open to innovative forms of testing.

Another drawback relates to possible limitations in technological capabilities and associated expenses. Obviously, having access to browser-based Web software tools becomes crucial at some point to make an Internet-based test feasible. The researcher developing a browser-based test needs both the resources and access to the Internet to keep data and scoring centralized. Participants and/or the person administering the test (if other than the researcher, as in a counseling center) would also need access to the Web in order to enter data and receive scoring results and feedback.

Another important issue is the matter of copyright, an unresolved difficulty in the emerging field of Internet publishing. A researcher who does not hold the copyright to the instrument that is to be converted to a Web form may be unable to obtain the copyright holder's consent to have it developed electronically. Generally, a copyright holder hopes to retain control of scoring and, if at all, may wish to develop electronic versions of instruments in-house. This issue, which can prove to be a huge obstacle to a researcher who wishes to develop a well-established instrument into an Internet-based version, may explain why only a limited number of well-established psychological tests have been converted to and used on the Internet.

Web testing, if done in the participant's home, would probably be unmonitored. As with unmonitored paper-and-pencil tests, cheating is possible. If a participant is motivated to take an Internet-based psychological test for education and guidance, however, the privacy factor may actually increase the veracity of responses concerning sensitive material, particularly if the test is taken anonymously (Kobak et al., 1996; Wolford & Rosenberg, 1998). On the other hand, Internet-based testing might not be applicable for involuntary, non-monitored situations, such as court ordered testing.

Although Web availability is growing every day, another disadvantage of using the Internet for research participants is that the numbers tested are likely to reflect the demographics of those populating the Web. On the other hand, if a researcher is studying a group with rare or special attributes, often these people can be located more easily on the Web through an e-mailing list, an Internet forum or chat group, where they can easily be contacted to administer a certain online test.

Along with a concern about research participants, there is always a possibility that test-takers may not read instructions properly or may ignore disclaimers, perhaps more frequently so than in monitored face-to-face situations. Also, participants may ignore, more than in a face-to-face testing situation, advice given to them to seek professional counseling. Monitoring a non-compliant subject can be difficult, even impossible, and needed support may be lacking in the case of a perceived failure or the existence of a psychological problem (these situations may also arise, though to a lesser degree, in face-to-face situations as well). This problem is associated with the fact that test-takers of Internet-based psychological tests are practically left alone in case of failure or what may be labeled as negative personality assessment. An extreme example might be of a person who gets results showing high suggestibility and suicide risk, who then goes on to commit suicide. This problem, obviously, does not exist when people are being tested in a clinical context.

Another problem has to do with the multiplicity of Internet-based psychological tests; it is often difficult to distinguish between legitimate, professional, measurement instruments and pop-culture "personality" quizzes, the latter being very common on the Internet. This leaves an open door for misuse if either test-taker or test administrator is unaware of the differences, especially if there is a service charge for use. It is important for a user taking an Internet-based psychological test do so from a reputable site and to be familiar with the instrument administered or, at least, be provided with full, relevant information on the psychometric quality of the test.

Another problem associated with online testing is related to one of the basic characteristics of the Internet, namely, borderless, global communication. Through the Internet, tests are easily available in many cultures other than the one where a test was developed and intended for. Test results may therefore not apply to test-takers outside the culture in which the test was standardized. While in the pre-Internet era this problem was relatively marginal, it has potentially become major at the present time.

Another drawback of using an Internet-based test has to do with still prevailing technological difficulties. Specifically, there is always the possibility that the client's browser, monitor, and/or video card may have other settings or an entirely different configuration than the designer intended, so that the layout of the questionnaire or test might look somewhat different from that envisioned. The user's software and hardware ultimately display the test or questionnaire, and the hosting Web server has no control over those versions, specifications, or settings. As a result, the designer of the test is best served by creating Web pages that are simple to display, using the most general, tried-and-true standards available so as to reach and serve as many varieties of client machines as possible. Related to this problem is the fact that Internet connection quality varies among users, depending on their own equipment as well as the equipment used by the service providers and other intersections along the information superhighway. A slow modem, a small screen, or a problematic phone line might significantly undermine online testing. This relates to a potential problem that arises when a test-taker has to restart a test, due to a technical failure, while there is no known way to control or adjust the test score for this abnormal test-taking procedure.

A major disadvantage of Internet-based testing relates to information security. A popular concern in the media is that data can be compromised through electronic "tapping" or hacking. Although this is possible, the expense and expertise needed to accomplish this task make it extremely unlikely that such tests and their results will be a target. To put this problem in perspective, this task would be akin to a government agency tapping one's phone, sitting outside one's building in a van or taking up residence in a nearby apartment with all sorts of expensive eavesdropping equipment, on the chance moment that there might be an opportunity to snag one's upload of an MBTI score. The data is actually no more at risk with Web technology than any data that resides on a computer. Moreover, there is no evidence that test data are more secure if paper-and-pencil tests are used and materials are archived in standard office cabinet files or drawers than on an Internet server. If normal security protocols concerning Web servers are used, there appears to be no greater risk for data collected on the Internet to be illegally obtained than any other electronic data or data saved on traditional paper materials. It should be noted, however, that only a negligible number of open testing websites use secured servers.

In summary, Internet-based testing and Web data collection have a number of advantages over paper-and-pencil testing. Many of the same disadvantages and cautions needed for paper testing, however, are also needed for electronic testing. Internet-based testing can in many ways be more secure than paper testing, but taking normal precautions would apparently make the former no less secure than the latter.

RESEARCH ON INTERNET-BASED PSYCHOLOGICAL TESTING

The relative newness of Internet-based testing does not permit a comprehensive review of the research, for the simple reason that this research is only in its infancy. A thorough review of the Internet and relevant professional databases revealed that there are very few published studies on Internet-based tests to date. In addition, those empirical investigations published have added very little knowledge to the limited information on this subject that was available several years ago (Schmidt, 1997).

Several central research questions may be asked in relation to Internet-based psychological testing: Is this procedure as reliable and valid as pencil-and-paper testing in this domain? Is this true for *all types* of estimates of the reliability of measurement and *all forms* of test validity? Are there testing areas, or specific tests, that are more suitable for Internet testing than others? What are the boundaries and specific limitations of Internet testing in terms of reliability and validity of measurement? What is the estimated utility of using Internet-based tests insofar as types of tests, testing purposes, available infrastructure, and other relevant variables? What technological means and procedures may enhance both measurement quality and users' satisfaction? As mentioned, very few answers are now available to several of these questions. The following is an overall review of what is currently available.

Smith and Leigh (1997) compared the results of a sexual fantasies survey administered through paper-and-pencil to 56 introductory psychology students and to 72 Web surfers who volunteered to fill out Internet-based questionnaires. The researchers found no significant differences between the two data sets. Furthermore, differences between men and women in the two samples replicated the differences found in the original study in which the questionnaire was developed.

Bicanich, Slivinski, Hardwicke, and Kapes (1997) reported on a research project in which an Internet-based vocational test battery and a parallel paper-and-pencil test battery were administered to two samples of secondary and post-secondary vocational-education students. No information was provided as to the nature of the tests other than their purpose, which was to evaluate vocational-related diagnostic measures. Bicanich et al. did not provide a detailed description of the findings, but they reported that the test results from the two versions were very similar and did not yield a bias related to gender or special educational needs (e.g., disability). They also found that students preferred Internet delivery to paper-and-pencil versions by a three-to-one margin. Bicanich et al. reported, furthermore, that the test administrators told of a significant saving in time and effort from Internet test delivery. In regard to financial utility, the economic parameters of their project showed that cost savings could be expected to accrue after 375 test-takers. Obviously, this datum should be considered meaningful in the context of the conditions of this specific project.

As a general rule, no psychological testing Website or online psychological test is accompanied by empirical research information concerning its measurement quality. An exception is the *QueenDom.Com* Website. Jerabek ("Cyberia Shrink," 1999) provides much psychometric information on a series of online tests available on this site. The tests include those for intelligence, relationship, personality, career/job, emotional health, and general knowledge in a number of areas. Psychometric information, based on large samples of test-takers and published on 14 of the tests on this website, supplies descriptive statistics, reliability estimates (i.e., internal consistency coefficients), norm tables (percentiles), and some comparisons or correlations relating to basic variables (e.g., age, gender). The psychometric information is quite impressive: all tests are nearly normally distributed, split-half and alpha coefficients are in the .90s, and relationships to external variables generally support high construct validity (e.g., positive correlations between Emotional IQ and professional success).

Stanton (1998) compared identical psychological survey questionnaires administered to two equivalent groups of "employed professionals" in either paper-and-pencil ($n = 181$) or Internet-based ($n = 50$) versions. Twelve items in the questionnaire measured respondents' perceptions of fairness in their day-to-day interactions with their supervisors, and a few others referred to demographic information and the nature of supervisory relations. Stanton found very similar results in the two samples in terms of the magnitude and internal structure of the items. The items in the Internet version, however, showed greater variability. Another noteworthy finding in this study was that there were significantly fewer missing values in the Internet version than in the paper-and-pencil version.

Pasveer and Ellard (1998) compared the administration of a 20-item self-trust questionnaire through paper-and-pencil and the Internet to two standard (n's of 760 and 148, respectively) and two Web-user (n's of 429 and 1,657, respectively) samples. Findings revealed that (a) both forms were similarly internally consistent (Cronbach alpha coefficients were .84 and .86 in the two standard samples, and .86 and .88 in the two Internet samples); (b) the two versions had a similar four-factor structure; (c) item means were similar in the two versions. The only meaningful difference occurred in the variance of the item responses, which was slightly higher in the Web version of the scale (mean item standard deviations of .56 and .60, and of .63 and .73, for the standard and the Internet administrations, respectively). This difference could be attributed, however, to the more heterogeneous sample responding to the Internet-based questionnaire.

Buchanan and Smith (1999a) compared a traditional paper-and-pencil version of a self-monitoring scale consisting of 18 dichotomous items to its Internet version. They found that the Web version ($n = 963$) had a coefficient alpha of .75, compared with .73 for the traditional-version comparison group ($n = 224$), and with .70 reported by earlier studies. A similar three-factor structure, similarly loaded by items, was found in the two versions. In addition, the mean scale scores and standard deviations of the two forms were similar. In an additional two studies, Buchanan and Smith (1999b) were able to provide evidence for validity of Internet-based testing of self-monitoring, using either Newsgroup participant's anonymity condition (Study 1, $n = 415$), or self-reported behaviors (Study 2, $n = 218$).

Pettit (1999) explored the possibility of using the Internet to collect psychological information. He launched a computer-anxiety scale on a university website, advertised it through Web search engines and indices, and asked Web surfers to fill it out. Analyses of 839 completed surveys showed that the scale was as internally consistent as the original paper-and-pencil scale. In addition, an examination of correlations of the scale with several other variables (e.g., age, gender, computer usage) showed that it possessed high construct validity.

Joinson (1999), in a 2×2 factorial design, examined whether conditions of anonymity (anonymous versus non-anonymous) and testing mode (paper-and-pencil versus Internet) might affect social desirability, social anxiety, and self-esteem scores in a sample of university students. He found that respondents who filled out questionnaires on the Internet, showed lower social desirability, lower social anxiety, and marginally higher self-esteem than did those tested by paper-and-pencil questionnaires. Similarly, the study participants scored lower on social desirability and social anxiety and higher on self-esteem in the anonymous than in the non-anonymous condition. As expected, the combination of anonymity and Internet-based testing resulted in the lowest social desirability scores. Joinson asserted that his research offered clear empirical support for the use of Internet-based self-reported psychological questionnaires, especially in an anonymous condition, as a better method to collect valid research data.

USES OF INTERNET-BASED PSYCHOLOGICAL TESTING

The numerous professional opportunities made available by Internet-based psychological tests almost guarantee that they will flourish with time as the Net becomes an everyday, routine tool for professionals and laymen alike. The combination of advantages enumerated above, together with convenience of usage and very positive feedback from empirical research, gives this new development great encouragement. It seems likely that Internet-based psychological tests will be used for various specific reasons and needs as professionals take advantage of growing computer capabilities, high-speed computer communications and related technologies, and the enormously growing prevalence of Internet users.

Internet-based psychological testing may be adopted in a number of ways and for a number of functions. First, being relatively simple and efficient to use, it is a tool of quality in *research data collection*. That is, researchers may use Internet-based tests–of their own or by linking to certain Web pages–in combination with other research variables (e.g., nature of participants employed, testing condition, differential instructions). Similarly, researchers may validly use Internet-based tests and questionnaires for survey research as has been shown in various investigations: Cooper, Scherer, Boies, and Gordon (1999) in a survey of Internet-sexuality-related behaviors through a questionnaire posted on *ABC*'s website; Kaye and Johnson (1999) for a political survey published on an independent website; and Greenfield's (1999) *MSNBC* survey on Internet addiction. Indeed, a growing number of ongoing psychological investigations are conducted online, using various kinds of Internet-based psychological tests and questionnaires. Examples of current projects: an anger-disorders survey (http://www.liii.com/~fantine/consent.html), an assessment of psychology investigation (http://www.unibw-hamburg.de/PWEB/psypae/eng.html), a study of marital relationships (http://www.unc.edu/~schaefer/mariint.htm), and research of social attri-butions   (http://www.geocities.com/CollegePark/Campus/3101/prism.htm). Joinson's (1999) findings, as mentioned above, support this method, based on a combination of Internet and anonymity, as a superior method for valid research data collection.

Second, Internet-based psychological tests may be used broadly for the sake of "mere" *self-knowledge, awareness, and insight*. That is, test-takers may complete different types of psychological tests or surveys and receive computerized numerical and narrative feedback that might provide a wide range of objective information about themselves. As discussed for the *QueenDom.com* website and related psychometric information (Jerabek, 1999), this procedure–at least from a psychometric perspective–may be very useful. One should not overlook, however, the great impact of test-takers' integrity, motivation, and obedience in determining the validity of an unmonitored, online test result. Nonetheless, Internet-based psychological assessment and testing may be of great service for individuals who prefer self-help resources to cope with personal concerns or debate specific questions (Tucker-Ladd, 1999, Ch. 15). Availability of and access to psychological tests made possible by the Internet–otherwise practically unavailable and/or inaccessible to non-professional people–may mark a new development for human services. A recent review by Oliver and Zack (1999) of 24 websites that offer career assessment tests, however, showed that most of them were rated mediocre in terms of professional quality. As the two researchers suggested, much work still remains to be done in order to improve the quality of these important services.

Third, Internet-based psychological tests may also provide efficient service to professionals–psychologists of different specialties, psychiatrists, clinical social workers, guidance counselors–who may *refer clients to a test readily available* on the Net as an integral component of the counseling or psychotherapeutic process. Such a psychological test or questionnaire may be completed at a place and time of the client's convenience, independent of and in addition to clinic time. For professionals, this option creates an opportunity to introduce a great variety of relevant tests into the counseling process, as well as to save costly clinic time and expense. For example, as noted by Gore and Leuwerke (2000), Davies, Turcotte, Hess, and Smithson (1997), Sampson (1999), and Stevens and Lundberg (1998), Internet-based self-assessments in career guidance can easily be integrated with career counseling services to complement other relevant Internet services, such as career information. Likewise, clinicians may take advantage of Internet-based psychological tests to make comprehensive, yet individually subscribed, diagnoses by using tests that are available on the Net, without having to keep updates of a large number of test forms. In this context, it should be mentioned that computerized clinical psychological tests have been found to be of much psychometric as well as practical value in clinical practice (Kobak et al., 1996).

A fourth possible use of Internet-based tests is for *candidate selection* (Bartram, 1997, 1999). Obviously, this option necessitates monitoring test-takers in order to prevent cheating and other forms of dishonest conduct. Nevertheless, allowing candidates to take tests through the Internet (under personal surveillance) has special advantages, like those of the aforementioned computerized tests, especially in regard to fast and accurate scoring. In addition, as the tests are centrally located and maintained, a testing agency does not have to worry about updated test versions and norms. Also, a testing agency may "own" a very broad spectrum of tests and scales from which to choose for a particular purpose (i.e., job or study program); the ones selected can then be administered to a group of relevant candidates. A step toward this direction was recently introduced by the Civil Service of the State of California (Coffee, Pearce, & Nishimura, 1999), which successfully delivered to candidates an application procedure together with a testing process through the Internet.

A fifth possible use of Internet-based psychological testing is for very *special assessment purposes* or for procedures that do not ordinarily exist in test libraries but may be found on and used through the Internet, such as testing variables relating to virtual reality and three-dimensional perception. Special computerized tests developed for this purpose and available on the Internet (Riva, 1998) can easily be of service. Again, a test taken from a remote location–for which, if desired, payment could also be collected online–saves the bother of using the regular mail, having to install a program on a local personal computer, or mastering administration and scoring procedures.

ETHICAL AND LEGAL CONSIDERATIONS

The Internet, as discussed by King (1999), is a typical form of anarchy. Hence, without enforced order and regulated operations, sensitive materials may easily be misused at the expense of innocent Web users. The nature of Internet-based psychological tests and testing procedures makes them quite fragile in terms of ethical standards. In fact, most ethical principles laid down by the American Psychological Association (1992) and its standards for psychological testing (1985) may easily be violated when psychological tests are offered online. Among obvious ethical problems is the lack of a clear context of "defined professional relationship"; the absence of ways to substantiate test findings and interpretations; the use of tests or test information by unqualified persons; the possibility of using tests that have not been strictly developed under appropriate scientific procedures; the lack (or partial lack) of information on reliability, validation, and other related information on tests; the limited ability to take appropriate information into account in interpreting test results and making professional judgments; the existence of tests that have been developed and/or are offered by unqualified persons; the use of outdated or obsolete tests; the possible limited ability to explain assessment results to test-takers; the problem of maintaining test security; the possible use of test results without obtaining test-takers' permission; and, not least the major problem, of assuring the secrecy of an individual's test results. On top of all of these ethical issues, there is the paramount issue of copyright. It is quite common to find psychological tests that were entirely or partially copied from copyrighted materials and published on Internet sites without permission or without even mentioning this point. Issues of copyright related to the Internet are complicated and are still undergoing legal construction. It seems, however, that the ease of publishing and distributing attractive testing materials through the Internet, while maintaining anonymity, presents a legal and law-enforcement challenge.

Numerous scholars have addressed concerns relating to the provision of psychological services over the Internet and have proposed various ways to deal with them (e.g., Bloom, 1998; Sampson, Kolodinsky, & Greeno, 1997; Tait, 1999). Direct reference to and analysis of issues related to testing and assessment, however, have yet to be proposed (Oliver & Zack, 1999). The Internet-related ethical guidelines available today from both the American Psychological Association (1999) and the National Board for Certified Counselors (1997), as two representative professional organizations, fail to *specifically* address this subject. In addition to the necessity for developing an appropriate ethical code, it is important to invest in educating professionals in relevant considerations (McMinn, Buchanan, Ellens, & Ryan, 1999). Also, there is a great need to expand our knowledge in all aspects of this area, such as computerized test interpretation (McMinn, Ellens, & Soref, 1999), in order to enable better professional and ethical judgments.

RECOMMENDATIONS FOR INTERNET-BASED PSYCHOLOGICAL TESTING

A huge number of psychological tests and scales, as mentioned, are published on the Internet. Many of these are open to the general public; that is, Internet users may test themselves (or suggest it to others; for instance, their children) and receive what is supposed to be professional feedback. This evolving technology in the service of the behavioral sciences has, as indicated above, special benefits. It eases the use of psychological measurement tools in social research; it provides a convenient vehicle for an individual's self-knowledge; it provides easy access to professionals who may need specific diagnostic tests for their work with certain clients; it allows efficient use of testing procedures in the assessment of job or education candidates (under certain conditions); and it enables the measurement of special human characteristics. These special benefits call for professional support and encouragement of the further development of Internet-based tests and testing procedures, on the one hand, and inviting and educating people to use these tests, on the other.

Yet, the lack of professional test-takers' monitoring of any kind makes this new reality problematic and, in extreme cases, even dangerous. As with other potentially problematic Internet services and functions and their related risks to users, multi-perspective solutions seem to be needed. Accordingly, it is necessary that relevant professional organizations and institutions develop a code of ethics and make it obligatory for their members. Although this solution would be applicable only to professionals (that is, non-professionals would be "free" to pursue their unethical testing on the Net), such a code could significantly reduce problematic Internet testing and enhance the quality of testing procedures. Another step—one that may increase the use of professional rather than non-professional testing sites—would be to adopt Ainsworth and Grohol's (1997) procedure for semi-licensing of Web counselors. These authors initiated a procedure in which Web counselors who meet certain criteria receive a logo—as a visible sign of their accreditation—which may appear on their websites. A similar device should be developed and offered for psychological testing sites that meet certain minimal standards.

Certainly, a massive effort should be made to examine the psychometric properties of Internet-based psychological tests. Test reliability and validity cannot be assumed to remain similar when converting a paper-and-pencil or even a personal computer test to an Internet version, as too many testing features are changed. This means that research and development should be a high priority. The intensive work of Jerabek (1999) on the many tests in the *QueenDom.Com* website should be commended, praised, and adopted.

Of no less importance, Web users ought to be educated on the actual usage of tests, from the very selection of an appropriate website, to examining a test's properties, and to understanding a test's limited results. This examination can be done through Internet portals, indices, and online guidance, and even embedded in general Internet training in schools. It would be helpful if professionals devoted time to publishing explanatory and educational articles on this issue in the general media, too.

The combination of these steps may further the quality of Internet-based psychological tests as well as foster their wiser use by Web surfers. Maximizing the benefits of Internet-based tests while minimizing their risks may prove a significant step forward for the behavioral sciences and indeed for humanity.

REFERENCES

Ainsworth, M., & Grohol, J. (1997). *Credentials check* [online]. Available (December, 1999): http://www.cmhc.com/check

American Psychological Association (1985). *Standards for educational and psychological testing.* Washington, DC: Author.

American Psychological Association (1992). *Ethical principles of psychologists and code of conduct.* Washington, DC: Author.

American Psychological Association (1997). *Services by telephone, teleconferencing, and Internet: A statement by the Ethics Committee of the American Psychological Association* [online]. Available (December, 1999): http://www.apa.org/ethics/stmnt01.html

Anderson, A. A. (1996). Predictors of computer anxiety and performance in information systems. *Computers in Human Behavior, 12*, 61-77.

Anderson, J. L. (1987). Computerized MAST for college health service. *Journal of American College Health, 36*, 83-88.

Ball, C. J., Scott, N., McLaren, P. M., & Watson, J. P. (1993). Preliminary evaluation of a Low-Cost VideoConferencing (LCVC) system for remote cognitive testing of adult psychiatric patients. *British Journal of Clinical Psychology, 32*, 303-307.

Barak, A. (1999). Psychological applications on the Internet: A discipline on the threshold of a new millennium. *Applied & Preventive Psychology, 8*, 231-246.

Bartram, D. (1997). Distance assessment: Psychological assessment through the Internet. *Selection and Development Review, 13 (3)*, 15-19.

Bartram, D. (1999). Testing and the Internet: Current realities, issues and future possibilities. *Selection and Development Review, 15 (6)*, 3-12.

Bicanich, E., Slivinski, T., Hardwicke, S. B., & Kapes, J. T. (1997). Internet-based testing: A vision or reality? *Technology Horizons in Education (T.H.E.) Journal.* [online]. Available (December, 1999): http://www.thejournal.com/magazine/vault/A1918.cfm

Bloom, J. W. (1998). The ethical practice of WebCounseling. *British Journal of Guidance and Counselling, 26,* 53-59.

Buchanan, T., & Smith, J. L. (1999a). Using the Internet for psychological research: Personality testing on the World Wide Web. *British Journal of Psychology, 90,* 125-144.

Buchanan, T., & Smith, J. L. (1999b). Research on the Internet: Validation of a World-Wide Web mediated personality scale. *Behavior Research Methods, Instruments, & Computers, 31,* 565-571.

Byers, A. P. (1981). Psychological evaluation by means of an online computer. *Behavior Research Methods & Instrumentation, 13,* 585-587.

Campbell, K. A., Rohlman, D. S., Storzbach, D., Binder, L. M., Anger, W. K., Kovera, C. A., Davis, K. L., & Grossman, S. J. (1999). Test-retest reliability of psychological and neurobehavioral tests self-administered by computer. *Assessment, 6,* 21-32.

Chua, S. L., Chen, D., & Wong, A. F. L. (1999). Computer anxiety and its correlates: A meta-analysis. *Computers in Human Behavior, 15,* 609-623.

Coffee, K., Pearce, J., & Nishimura, R. (1999). State of California: Civil service testing moves into cyberspace. *Public Personnel Management, 28,* 283-300.

Cooper, A., Scherer, C. R., Boies, S. C., & Gordon, B. L. (1999). Sexuality on the Internet: From sexual exploration to pathological expression. *Professional Psychology: Research & Practice, 30,* 154-164.

Davis, G., Turcotte, M., Hess, P., & Smithson, S. (1997). New approaches in delivery in the Canadian employment service. *Journal of Employment Counseling, 34,* 146-156.

DiLalla, D. L. (1996). Computerized administration of the Multidimensional Personality Questionnaire. *Assessment, 3,* 365-374.

Dyck, J. L., Gee, N. R., & Smither, J. A. (1999). The changing construct of computer anxiety for younger and older adults. *Computers in Human Behavior, 14,* 61-77.

English, N. (1996, October). *Web exams and surveys: Using the Web to gather and disseminate information.* Paper presented in Association for Computing Machinery/Special Interest Group on University and College Computing Services User Services Conference (SIGUCCS), Chicago.

English, N. (1997, November). *Using Web-based questionnaires.* Paper presented in the Society for Computers in Psychology Annual Conference, Philadelphia.

Gore, P. A., Jr., & Leuwerke, W. C. (2000). Information technology for career assessment on the Internet. *Journal of Career Assessment, 8,* 3-19.

Greenfield, D. N. (1999, August). Nature of Internet addiction: Psychological factors in compulsive Internet use. In B. L. Gordon & M. M. Maheu (Co-Chairs), *New findings on effects of Internet use.* Symposium conducted at the 107th Annual Convention of the American Psychological Association, Boston.

Harvey, R. J., & Hammer, A. L. (1999). Item response theory. *The Counseling Psychologist, 27,* 353-383.

Jerabek, I. (1999). *Body-mind QueenDom.Com* [online]. Available (December, 1999): http://www.queendom.com

Joinson, A. (1999). Social desirability, anonymity, and Internet-based questionnaires. *Behavior Research Methods, Instruments, & Computers, 31,* 433-438.

Kaye, B. K., & Johnson, T. J. (1999). Research methodology: Taming the cyber frontier: Techniques for improving online surveys. *Social Science Computer Review, 17,* 323-337.

King, S. A. (1999). Internet gambling and pornography: Illustrative examples of the psychological consequences of communication anarchy. *CyberPsychology & Behavior, 2,* 175-193.

Kingsbury, G. G., & Houser, R. L. (1999). Developing computerized adaptive tests for school children. In F. Drasgow & J. B. Olson-Buchanan (Eds.), *Innovations in computerized assessment* (pp. 93-115). Mahwah, NJ: Erlbaum.

Kobak, K. A., Greist, J. H., Jefferson, J. W., & Katzelnick, D. J. (1996). Computer-administered clinical rating scales: A review. *Psychopharmacology, 127,* 291-301.

Lankford, J. S., Bell, R. W., & Elias, J. W. (1994). Computerized versus standard personality measures: Equivalency, computer anxiety, and gender differences. *Computers in Human Behavior, 10,* 497-510.

McMinn, M. R., Buchanan, T., Ellens, B. M., & Ryan, M. K. (1999). Technology, professional practice, and ethics: Survey findings and implications. *Professional Psychology: Research and Practice, 30,* 165-172.

McMinn, M. R., Ellens, B. M., & Soref, E. (1999). Ethical perspectives and practice behaviors involving computer-based test interpretations. *Assessment, 6,* 71-77.

Meijer, R. R., & Nering, M. L. (1999). Computerized adaptive testing: Overview and introduction. *Applied Psychological Measurement, 23,* 187-194.

Miles, E. W., & King, W. C., Jr. (1998). Gender and administration mode effects when paper-and-pencil personality tests are computerized. *Educational & Psychological Measurement, 58,* 68-76.

National Board for Certified Counselors (1997). *Standards for the Ethical Practice of WebCounseling* [online]. Available (February, 1999): http://www.nbcc.org/ethics/wcstandards.htm

Neuman, G., & Baydoun, R. (1998). Computerization of paper-and-pencil tests: When are they equivalent? *Applied Psychological Measurement, 22,* 71-83.

Oliver, L. W., & Zack, J. S. (1999). Career assessment on the Internet: An exploratory study. *Journal of Career Assessment, 7,* 323-356.

Pasveer, K. A., & Ellard, J. H. (1998). The making of a personality inventory: Help from the WWW. *Behavior Research Methods, Instruments, & Computers, 30,* 309-313.

Pettit, F. A. (1999). Exploring the use of the World Wide Web as a psychology data collection tool. *Computers in Human Behavior, 15,* 67-71.

Riva, G. (1998). Virtual reality in psychological assessment: The body image virtual reality scale. *CyberPsychology & Behavior, 1,* 37-44.

Russell, M. (1999). Testing on computers: A follow-up study comparing performance on computer and on paper. *Education Policy Analysis Archives, 7 (20)* [online]. Available (October, 1999): http://epaa.asu.edu/epaa/v7n20

Russell, M., & Haney, W. (1997). Testing writing on computers: An experiment comparing student performance on tests conducted via computer and via paper-and-pencil. *Education Policy Analysis Archives, 5 (3)* [online]. Available (October, 1999): http://olam.ed.asu.edu/epaa/v5n3.html

Sampson, J. P., Jr. (1990). Computer-assisted testing and the goals of counseling psychology. *The Counseling Psychologist, 18,* 227-239.

Sampson, J. P., Jr. (1999). Integrating Internet-based distance guidance with services provided in career centers. *Career Development Quarterly, 47,* 243-254.

Sampson, J. P., Jr., Kolodinsky, R. W., & Greeno, B. P. (1997). Counseling on the information highway: Future possibilities and potential problems. *Journal of Counseling and Development, 75,* 203-212.

Schmidt, W. C. (1997). World Wide Web survey research: Benefits, potential problems, and solutions. *Behavior Research Methods, Instruments, & Computers, 29,* 274-279.

Smith, M. A., & Leigh, B. (1997). Virtual subjects: Using the Internet as an alternative source of subjects and research environments. *Behavior Research Methods, Instruments, & Computers, 30,* 526-537.

Stanton, J. M. (1998). An empirical assessment of data collection using the Internet. *Personnel Psychology, 51,* 709-725.

Stevens, D. T., & Lundberg, D. J. (1998). The emergence of the Internet: Enhancing career counseling education and services. *Journal of Career Development, 24,* 195-208.

Tait, A. (1999). Face-to-face and at a distance: The mediation of guidance and counselling through the new technologies. *British Journal of Guidance & Counselling, 27,* 113-122.

Tucker-Ladd, C. E. (1999). *Psychological self-help* [online]. Available (December, 1999): http://mentalhelp.net/psyhelp

Turner, C. F., Ku, L., Rogers, S. M., Lindberg, L. D., Pleck, J. H., & Sonenstein, F. L. (1998). Adolescent sexual behavior, drug use, and violence: Increased reporting with computer survey technology. *Science, 280,* 867-873.

Wolford, G. L., & Rosenberg, S. (1998, November). *Computerized data collection from SMI.* Paper presented in the Society for Computers in Psychology Annual Conference, Dallas.

Zickar, M. J., Overton, R. C., Taylor, L. R., & Harms, H. J. (1999). The development of a computerized selection system for computer programmers in a financial services company. In F. Drasgow & J. B. Olson-Buchanan (Eds.), *Innovations in computerized assessment* (pp. 7-33). Mahwah, NJ: Erlbaum.

Walking Through the Fire:
Integrating Technology to Enhance
the Research Skills of Minority
Mental Health Student Researchers

Philip M. Ouellette
Richard Briscoe

SUMMARY. The information technology revolution and the "communication age" have brought many new and challenging imperatives for educators and researchers interested in the enhancement of community-based human service delivery systems in mental health. A technology-supported training environment is described to enhance the development of research skills of undergraduate level multicultural mental health researchers. *[Article copies available for a fee from The Haworth Document Delivery Service: 1-800-HAWORTH. E-mail address: <getinfo@haworthpressinc.com> Website: <http://www.HaworthPress.com> © 2002 by The Haworth Press, Inc. All rights reserved.]*

Philip M. Ouellette, PhD, is Assistant Professor at the Louis de la Parte Florida Mental Health Institute, Department of Child and Family Studies and School of Social Work, University of South Florida, 4202 E. Fowler Avenue MGY 132, Tampa, FL 33620 (E-Mail: pouelet@chuma1.cas.usf.edu).

Richard Briscoe, PhD, is Assistant Professor at the Louis de la Parte Florida Mental Health Institute, Department of Child and Family Studies, 13301 Bruce B. Downs Blvd., Tampa, FL 33621 (E-Mail: briscoe@hal.fmhi.usf.edu).

[Haworth co-indexing entry note]: "Walking Through the Fire: Integrating Technology to Enhance the Research Skills of Minority Mental Health Student Researchers." Ouellette, Philip M., and Richard Briscoe. Co-published simultaneously in *Journal of Technology in Human Services* (The Haworth Press, Inc.) Vol. 19, No. 2/3, 2002, pp. 91-107; and: *Using the Internet as a Research Tool for Social Work and Human Services* (ed: Goutham M. Menon) The Haworth Press, Inc., 2002, pp. 91-107. Single or multiple copies of this article are available for a fee from The Haworth Document Delivery Service [1-800-HAWORTH, 9:00 a.m. - 5:00 p.m. (EST). E-mail address: getinfo@haworthpressinc.com].

KEYWORDS. Technology-supported instruction, mental health research, training, multicultural, Internet-based training

INTRODUCTION

Computer and telecommunications technologies are becoming a vital communication medium throughout our society. Computer usage, e-mail and Internet use, and home purchases of computers are growing rapidly (Gonzalez, 1995; Katz & Aspden, 1997). As a result, the information technology revolution and the "communication age" have brought many new and challenging imperatives for educators and researchers interested in the enhancement of community-based human service delivery systems in Children's Mental Health. As new technologies continue to be integrated in the human service field, the ways we teach, learn, and conduct research are also changing. Because of advances in technology, an opportunity exists for educators and researchers to enhance training opportunities for minority mental health researchers and professionals.

The percentage of American-born minority students who choose research science careers is disproportionately low compared with the number of students in the general population who choose scientific careers. Minority professionals are underrepresented at all levels of science research careers. Trained and funded minority researchers are inadequately represented in children's mental health. Traditionally, programs training practitioners have placed very little emphasis on research skills (Pfeiffer & Marmo, 1981; Shinn, 1987). Of the studies assessing students' perception of research training, more than 70% reported little emphasis on research training. Shulman (1981) has suggested that not only should research be emphasized in training programs but students should be trained in more than one research method. The goal should be to train students on a wider variety of research methods that they can apply to various situations (Goldman, 1979; Wampold, 1986). Wampold (1986) has suggested that research training should emphasize didactic training as well as experiential training. While the first one is typically learned in a classroom setting, the second can be accomplished by participating in ongoing research.

A technology-supported learning environment was integrated within the Multicultural Mental Health Training Program (MMHTP), a training program specifically designed to meet the needs of young minority children mental health researchers. The Multicultural Mental Health

Training Program (MMHTP) is unique from most other research training programs as it recognizes the importance of increasing the number of underrepresented multicultural researchers dedicated to understanding and studying the mental health needs of children in an increasingly ethnically diverse population. The importance of developing a training context that facilitates the mentoring and support of minority students and the importance of training researchers in acquiring the necessary research skills and methods are a cornerstone of this program. This training program presents multiple innovative approaches, including the use of technology, to give minority students an awareness of the behavioral research that is conducted as well as to provide an appreciation for the research skills needed for careers in the field. MMHTP recognizes the importance of computer technology as a medium that can be used for both training purposes and for conducting research. The Web-based instructional medium provides a unique context for enhancing professional networking and mutual support among minority students, which is sometimes difficult in a traditional training context. The electronic medium is also useful for the development and monitoring of student individual goals and for monitoring ongoing program evaluation. Through multiple technology-supported instructional approaches and carefully designed action-learning activities, opportunities exist for minority student researchers to gain an appreciation for the power of the Internet and communication technology. The use of a technology-supported learning environment can be a useful medium for learning how to conduct socially significant research that impacts the everyday lives of children and families and their communities.

This article describes how a technology-supported training environment can be used to enhance the development of research skills of minority researchers in the children's mental health field. The Web-based training environment that was integrated into a traditionally taught mental health research training program, provided a unique context for experiencing the actual research process as well as providing for the necessary supports that the beginning researcher requires. By providing a virtual learning environment for complementing traditionally presented didactic training seminars, minority student researchers can not only readily access the support needed but can also develop research skills for implementing a variety of applied research projects. In an electronic learning medium, the potential exists for the development of an ongoing interdisciplinary collaborative network of ethnic minority mental health researchers while at the same time enhancing Internet-based research activities and projects. The following will describe the rationale for the development of a Web-based learning environment and a description of how it was integrated into the Multicultural Mental Health Training Program to enhance the program's training objectives. Implications for training mental health researchers and lessons learned from an Internet-based instructional environment are reviewed.

TECHNOLOGY-SUPPORTED LEARNING ENVIRONMENTS

Moving towards learning paradigms and cooperative learning environments. Teachers who successfully use technology function more as instructional designers than lesson planners. This is especially true when they seek to incorporate computer-mediated innovations, such as the use of telecommunication tools into existing classroom-based curriculums (Harris, 1998). Communication technologies are tools that are applied in many different settings. Applying these tools into existing curriculum activities most often requires instructional innovation. Moving from a classroom-based learning environment to an electronic medium requires a major shift in the way we think about teaching and the way students learn.

The gradual shift occurring in many educational settings today is towards a paradigm that recognizes the educational institution as existing primarily to facilitate learning by whatever means necessary. As more emphasis is placed on the importance of learning outcomes, learning changes from a teacher-driven process, referred to as an instructional paradigm where the instructor is the primary source of new information, to an environment where the learner is increasingly empowered to direct his or her own learning process. In this new paradigm, referred to as a learning paradigm (Barr & Tagg, 1995), the role of the educator shifts from primary instructor to more of a guide in the learning journey of students. Through ongoing peer interaction and collaborative learning strategies, students are empowered to take charge of their own learning as they discover knowledge for themselves, making learning a student-driven process. The use of collaborative learning strategies (Nixon, 1998) supports the gradual shift toward a learning versus an instructional paradigm. Collaborative learning strategies have been found to increase student motivation and achievement while promoting greater use of higher-level reasoning strategies and critical thinking. Educational researchers have found that collaborative learning environments create a sense of social cohesion as well as facilitate productive learning (Abrami et al., 1995; Johnson et al., 1991; Slavin, 1991).

Designing a technology-mediated learning environment appears to be well suited for the educator adhering to an educational paradigm that favors student-driven learning. Because of the improvement of several new instructional software programs, instruction can be delivered to students on campus, in their homes, or in their work places (Baker & Gloster, 1994). The idea of implementing a technology-supported learning environment such as the "Virtual Classroom" as a viable added dimension to the learning process for training human service professionals has been explicated elsewhere (Ouellette, 1999). Additionally, scholars and proponents of technology-supported learning advocate the use of collaborative learning as an important component of Internet-based instruction. Some have argued that combinations of new computer technologies that facilitate collaboration and communication among learners can support and enhance learning, particularly in distance learning environments (Pea, 1993). Research results bear out the premise that electronic networking can improve self-efficacy. Several studies have found that students who work in a networked environment have many benefits that their non-networked partners do not experience (Waugh & Rath, 1995). These benefits include: emotional support from peers, feedback on pedagogical and teaching techniques, promotion of reflection and effective peer dialogue and facilitative means of communication with instructors and supervisors (Mathew et al., 1998).

Factors important to designing technology-supported learning environments. In designing technology-supported learning environments, it was found that one could not simply transfer classroom-designed teaching materials into a technology-mediated learning environment. Not all classroom-designed teaching and learning strategies are necessarily conducive to or even appropriate for a technology-supported learning environment. For example, the inclusion of a dynamic lecture presentation by an animated presenter in a traditional classroom setting may actually seem excessively long and tedious for the learner when the lecture is simply transcribed in a text format within a technology-supported learning environment. The issue of maintaining high quality, student-centered learning activities, involving small group interaction and experiential learning was found to be of utmost importance when designing a technology-supported learning environment. Essentially, a technology-supported learning environment involves designing a series of active learning tasks (Misale et al., 1996; Hollingsworth et al., 1998) that provide students with the opportunity to not only acquire new information from a variety of sources, but to interact with peers and instructors about their evolving thought processes. The technology-supported learning environment allows this to occur without the barriers of meeting in fixed locations and in accordance with rigid time schedules.

The adoption of technological innovations into existing curriculums is an active process that involves much reinvention. Teaching strategies must "fit" or be adaptive to the teaching medium being used. Creating a successful technology-mediated learning environment requires that educators design instructional activities that employ the communication tools available through technology in unique, personalized ways. For example, the use of e-mail is becoming a useful tool for enhancing personal contact between student and instructor. The educators must take the new tool and "make it their own" if regular use of the innovation is to continue (Harris, 1998). However, as one moves from a traditional teaching format to an online environment, resistance to engage in this new learning environment can be expected both from students and instructors alike. Many factors contribute to the success or failure of any kind of innovation. These include the lack of information about the innovation being introduced. Another is unclear messages regarding the need for this new teaching and learning format, and unclear expectations regarding new roles and responsibilities that will evolve from a new teaching and learning environment. Another factor that may contribute to resistance is inadequate reassurances of the individual's ability to be successful in engaging in this new learning environment. Some educators have suggested a few guidelines that enable students to move toward a successful transition to a new online learning environment. The following are examples:

- Ensure there is an adequate adjustment period to this new method of learning;
- Monitor students' progress and provide external motivation support when needed;
- Provide a mechanism for students to self-monitor their progress and engagement levels;
- Ensure students have adequate equipment to fully utilize the features and functionality of the online environment (Ullrich, 1998).

When transitioning from a traditional training environment to a technology-supported medium, the issue of maintaining high quality, student-centered learning activity is considered to be of utmost importance. That is, students are provided learning activities that permit learning at an individualized pace rather than in a competitive group atmosphere often found in a traditional classroom setting. For this reason, a conscious effort must be made to assure collaboration among students and instructors. If the course activities in a technology-supported learning environment do not facilitate active learning or if the teaching strategies rely totally on a passive "lecture-type" method, or students are only "spoon fed" a multitude of information, the technology-supported instructional delivery method will not necessarily translate into quality teaching and learning (Nixon, 1998).

Others have experienced positive outcomes when introducing technology-supported instruction to their students. Some of the positive outcomes reported were the shifts in the dynamics of learning from a teacher-centered, lecture-driven learning mode to a learner-centered, self-regulated, and needs-driven learning mode. More time appears to be available in a technology learning environment to develop a higher level of cognitive skills. Another factor contributing to positive outcomes includes the opportunity for students to participate in the construction of their own knowledge through the medium's conduciveness to cooperative learning. Cooperative learning is facilitated by the immediate feedback students can acquire from their instructor and their peers (Lan, 1999).

THE MULTICULTURAL MENTAL HEALTH PROGRAM

Overview of the Multicultural Mental Health Training Program (MMHTP). The State Legislature authorized the development of a culturally-based mental health professional training program at our University in 1987. The bill proposed a training program emphasizing practical techniques applicable to mental health service delivery in minority communities. The purpose of the program is "to increase the number of minority group members in the mental health professions who address the mental health needs of minority communities of the state." The MMHTP program provides mentoring, support, and training to individuals interested in pursuing a career in the mental health field. The primary mission of MMHTP is to develop a training model that increases the number of ethnic and culturally sensitive researchers traditionally underrepresented in mental health graduate school programs (Briscoe, Sedberry, & Henderson, 1996).

Success in conducting research requires graduate students to become actively involved in actual research experiences. However, undergraduate students, and particularly minority students, rarely have the opportunity to become involved in research projects, and as a result, they do not gain interest and the skills to conduct basic research activity. In order to provide minority students with an opportunity to acquire structured research experiences, the MMHTP program engages students in research practicum experiences and research training activities.

Student research training components. What makes MMHTP unique to other research training programs is its emphasis on four areas of skill development. The first is the development of close mentoring relationships. The second is the development of professional networks. The third is the development of specific career development skills. The fourth is the development of multi-methods research skills. The training approach used for initiating undergraduate minority students to careers in mental health research consists of a two-semester internship placement at the mental health research institute. A full-time internship program consists of 40 hours of work per week and a part-time internship program consists of 20 hours of work per week. Students receive a stipend for living and tuition expenses. Students participate in weekly group training seminars and other training activities with MMHTP staff. In addition, training consists of a research practicum where students are actively involved in ongoing research projects within the research Institute. Through multiple training components, promising minority students discover the importance of research skills as well as gain behavioral research experience.

Primary instructional medium. The two primary instructional mediums used for the development of research skills in the MMHTP training program have traditionally been the use of weekly group seminars and the research practicum. The group seminars involve weekly eight-hour face-to-face meetings, with training modules focusing on issues of research methodology, literature reviews, professional and career development training, and cultural competence. A unique component of the MMHTP training program is the professional and career development training modules. Professional and career development was found to be an essential component of training within mental health and related fields (Ducheny, Alletzhauser, Crandell, & Schneider, 1997; Miller, 1992; Skovholt & Ronnestad, 1992). The professional and career development training modules focus on students' advancement in mental health research careers. Invited university faculty facilitate round-table interactive seminars on topics that enhance the overall development of students' success in nonacademic areas necessary for degree completion, broadening students' conceptualization of professional experiences and career goals. Opportunities are provided for students to increase student-faculty interactions with university faculty.

Student Individual Training Plan (SITP). A basic training strategy used in the program is the utilization of individualized instruction. One of the most important aspects of the training program is the *Student Individual Training Plan (SITP).* It specifically requires students to identify and define individual training goals and an action plan. For many students who have never reflected upon writing long- and short-term goals, this provides an opportunity for students to articulate clearly defined goals and objectives. Students participate in a series of SITP activities to identify their strengths and areas for improvement in order to learn research skills. The SITP allows students the opportunity to develop individualized goals based on interests and needs. In addition, the SITP approach involves students in the self-monitoring of their goals, timelines, and activities.

Cultural diversity. Another unique aspect of the MMHTP program has been the inclusion of cultural diversity seminars integrated within the weekly seminar series. Cultural diversity seminars are designed to increase students' ability to improve service delivery to research and service delivery to ethnically and racially diverse populations. Seminar-based training sessions focus on students' self-awareness, knowledge of culture and its functions and ethnicity, and their learning to recognize and ameliorate cultural barriers to service delivery effectiveness. University faculty and community members involved in research and service in minority settings discuss topics relevant to ethnic-specific research.

Parallel with the weekly seminar series is the use of a research practicum in which the students actively participate in a hands-on research experience through a supervised opportunity to apply the knowledge they learned during the training seminars. Students are assigned to a faculty mentor for 12 hours per week for a part-time experience or 32 hours per week for a full-time experience. The faculty mentor engages the student in various research activities ranging from conceptualization and design to analysis and dissemination. One of the barriers to undergraduate students' developing research skills is their unfamiliarity with how basic methods of research are applied. Little or no experience in conducting actual research is available from most other research training programs. Undergraduate students in the MMHTP program are able to gain highly valuable research experience by participating in applied research projects. This hands-on research experience for undergraduate students was found to be helpful in obtaining graduate school admission by working with faculty on research projects (Plante, 1998; McDonald, 1997; Gibson, Kahn, & Mathie, 1996; Dunn & Toedter, 1991). The experience and knowledge gained from the research practicum is with respect to specific research tasks, such as the development of coding schemes, the refinement of instruments as well as the piloting of research instruments.

INTEGRATING A TECHNOLOGY-SUPPORTED LEARNING ENVIRONMENT TO ENHANCE RESEARCH SKILLS

Introducing a technology-supported learning environment into a highly structured and traditionally taught research training program is a challenge not only for instructors but for students as well. One way we facilitated its integration was to begin by focusing on the strengths of the MMHTP training program while adhering to its philosophical orientation and purpose; that is, its emphasis on the development of mentoring relationships, the inclusion of multiple research resources available from the institute's research setting, and MMHTP's opportunities for collaborative learning among peers. Using traditional training formats, barriers of time, distance, and availability of professional resources at designated times to fit specific student training schedules have been problematic.

The communication tools available on a technology-supported learning environment increase opportunities for frequent student and faculty exchanges. In addition, the electronic medium discourages the use of a "lecture-type" educational format when integrating materials within this environment. This minimizes spoon-feeding approaches to teaching and learning. A technology-supported training environment favors the inclusion of cooperative learning pedagogical strategies where learning is greatly facilitated.

Examples of Web-based learning activities. Guidelines offered by Ullrich (1998) were considered when designing learning activities for a technology-enhanced learning environment. One area considered essential to ensure successful participation of students in a technology-supported learning environment was to provide opportunities for proper orientation early in the training process. Learning to learn in this new environment requires a period of adjustment for most students as well as faculty. For example, to ensure there was an adequate adjustment period for students and faculty to adapt to this new way of teaching and learning, a series of mini-exercises were developed to assist faculty and students in learning how to use the various communication tools available in a technology-supported environment. Mini-orientation exercises were developed to guide faculty and students to learn about how to appropriately use synchronous communications such as a chat room, or non-synchronous communication tools such as an electronic discussion forum, and electronic mail. Our experience has found that an insufficient orientation period can lead to frustration and discourage future participation by all who participate in a technology-supported instructional and learning environment.

Another area for which the electronic medium was found to be useful was in the development of mentoring relationships, an important characteristic of MMHTP. For students to frequently interact with their assigned mentors through traditional means meant scheduling face-to-face meetings at specified times and locations making it difficult for busy research faculty members and students. The frequent use of e-mail between mentor and student allowed for more frequent contact between seminar sessions thus providing increased opportunities for needed guidance and support when needed. This increased communication capacity also provided an opportunity for a better constructive use of face-to-face seminar meetings as well as providing indicators for monitoring the quality of developing mentoring relationships between assigned research faculty and students.

The use of a weekly electronic personal learning journal is another interactive instrument used to monitor student progress with respect to their individualized training plan (SITP) and encourage student-faculty interaction. In a traditional instructional environment, students are asked to post periodic entries in a written personal journal regarding learning objectives worked on, actions or projects being worked on, and reactions to seminar training content. Journal entries are submitted to the faculty mentor on assigned dates or prior to certain scheduled meetings or seminar sessions. Submissions were often late or insufficiently completed. Responses from faculty mentors were often delayed due to busy research schedules or tardy submissions. The weekly electronic personal learning journal allowed students to post their entries at any time of day or night and forward to their faculty mentors from their own homes. Submissions of personal learning journals to the faculty mentors were found to be more consistent and responses from faculty mentors more immediate. The use of this teaching and learning tool served to enhance student-mentor relationships as well as to provide a means for monitoring progress.

Another important aspect of MMHTP is the opportunity for the development of peer support and peer-to-peer interaction. Collaborative learning opportunities among peers are considered an important instructional characteristic in the development of ongoing research career interests and in the development of research skills. In a traditional learning environment, opportunities for peer interaction are limited to seminar meetings. The extent to which peer interaction takes place is largely influenced by the instructional method used by individual faculty members presenting the various training modules. Not all instructors favor the use of active learning strategies when presenting training content, making peer interaction inconsistent and unpredictable. Electronic discussion forums facilitate increased use of peer-to-peer interaction as well as provide a context for collaborative learning. For example, student interns are assigned to small group discussion teams where they are to post reactions and comments on their team's discussion forum to questions posted by various instructors and invited guests to seminar meetings. This allows for a variety of discussion threads to develop on specific research themes and issues addressed in the MMHTP training modules, such as issues of career development, research methods, and cultural diversity. The input student researchers provide through discussion forums can be accessed at any time of day or night and at the convenience of all student interns and research faculty.

The MMHTP program makes use of a variety of mental health research faculty and other resources within the research institute to address various research-training issues. Traditionally, the seminar format is the primary forum used to provide these unique learning opportunities for students in MMHTP. Due to the limitation of restricted time and travel schedules of many researchers, such presentations are at times difficult to coordinate. The use of other synchronous communication environments such as the research chat room, allows for special guests and research specialists to participate in student-faculty discussions from a distance. Not only are resources of the Institute available to students but the research chat room allows for expert researchers from all parts of the country to contribute to the learning opportunities of student interns. This increases opportunities for professional networking among minority and culturally sensitive researchers which is one goal of MMHTP.

MMHTP's research skill development curriculum provides students with an opportunity to develop introductory computer skills, learn how to execute literature searches, and how to present findings. The electronic medium was especially conducive to introduce self-directed learning activities regarding the use of basic computer software while maintaining a training theme of research skill development. A number of self-directed learning pedagogical strategies specifically designed for the electronic medium were developed for the technology-supported learning environment. For example, students are provided with online projects on conducting Internet-based literature searches as well as exploring research database resources available through the University's virtual library or Internet search engines. In addition, basic computer skills can be acquired from structured Web-based learning assignments where students can enhance their skills in the use of word processing, databases, charting, statistical, and presentation software. Web-based learning assignments on the development of basic computer skills can be completed at a student's own pace and be focused on individualized skill levels.

CONCLUSIONS

Lessons learned from the project to date. An important initial finding in designing a technology-supported learning environment is the amount of time required to convert content-specific materials into a technology-supported teaching and learning environment. Despite the ease which some server-based instructional software provides to transfer materials to an Internet-based environment (Wernet et al., 1998), the instructor must have sufficient knowledge of the software, HTML code, and basic Web page design to prepare and edit the course materials placed on a course Web site. A novice or even a faculty member with reasonable technology-related instructional experience needs to acquire sufficient training or technical support to properly use Web-based instructional software.

Also unanticipated was the amount of time that was required to design learning assignments compatible to the medium and follow-up methods necessary to monitor student involvement. After each learning assignment, students provide immediate feedback regarding the clarity of assigned tasks. Their input suggests the importance of clearly defined instructions, estimated time frames for completing tasks, and due dates. In addition, when students are requested to communicate their ideas either in the personal learning journal or in a class discussion forum, it is important that messages are responded to as soon as possible. Too much delay between the time students' posting of a message and the time feedback is provided appears to hinder the quality of the learning process in a technology-supported instructional environment. To successfully engage students in a technology-supported learning environment, it was found important to make expectations clear as to the roles and responsibilities. It was found useful to specify estimated time frames and due dates when designing online learning assignments.

Another factor considered important in facilitating a successful transition to a technology-supported learning environment is the liberal and frequent use of student reassurances as they confront technical challenges. One of the most significant changes for both the research faculty and the student in an Internet-based learning environment is a shift in roles. For the student, his role changes from a passive recipient in the learning process to an active collaborator. That is, the student provides instant feedback regarding the nature of an assigned learning task due to the student's ready access to the instructor via e-mail, making learning much more of a student-driven and needs-determined process. For the instructor, the role shifts from that of teacher and the sole provider of new information to that of a designer of a learning context. Resources and research information can be acquired from a variety of sources through an Internet-based teaching and learning environment. By constantly adjusting and reinventing new and challenging medium-specific active-learning tasks, the instructor spends considerable time in the preparation of materials relevant to the research skill development needs of students.

Future directions. Integrating a technology-supported learning environment in a traditionally taught research training program has revealed numerous potentials and produced further challenges. To improve the work that has begun with this teaching and learning project, more work needs to be done in several areas. The following is suggested for future directions:

- Increase the participation and presence of research mentors on the course Web site especially with online discussion forums on relevant research skill development themes.
- Design more medium-specific active-learning tasks that require students to collaborate with one another and produce end products. A series of end products and the acquisition of clearly defined short-term objectives provide the necessary tools to encourage progress and provide feedback as to evolving research skills.
- Provide increased opportunities for students to interact with one another using the Web-based communication tools. Frequent interaction among peers and members of the faculty appears to cre-

ate the necessary supportive environment required of minority students involved in a research-training program. It also appears to largely contribute to the quality of the students' understanding of the overall research process.

- The electronic medium is relatively new to the mental health research student as a learning environment. The medium demands a major shift in the way we provide information to students and in the way students integrate newly developed skills. The medium appears more conducive to self-directed learning styles. There is, however, a strong tendency to revert to traditional teaching and learning styles when students and instructors are confronted with the struggles associated with too many technical difficulties. It is important to provide instructors and students with sufficient technical supports if technology is to be successfully integrated into existing research curricula.

One of the surprises for integrating a technology-supported learning environment into an existing mental health research training program has been the positive response of students. The medium appears to help fulfill their need to articulate their evolving thought processes as they are introduced to various research issues. The opportunity to interact with one another and to access the information and learning activities at their convenience appears to provide a greater sense of involvement in their own learning. We can conclude from this experience that integrating the use of a Web-based learning environment can enhance that student participation in the learning of research skills, provide a useful context for peer support, enhance student-mentor relationships, and can serve to complement traditionally taught research training seminars.

REFERENCES

Abrami, P. C., Chambers, B., Poulsen, C., De Simone, C., d'Apollonia, S., & Howden, J. (1995) *Classroom connections: Understanding and using cooperative learning.* Toronto, Ontario: Harcourt-Brace.

Baker, W., & Gloster, A. (1994) Moving towards the virtual university: A vision of technology in higher education. *Cause Effect, 17* (2), 4-11.

Barr, R., & Tagg, J. (1995) From teaching to learning: A new paradigm for undergraduate education. *Change, 27,* (6), 12-26.

Briscoe, R.V., Sedberry, G., & Henderson, E. (1996). *Multicultural Mental Health Training Program (MMHTP): A comprehensive training program for improving service delivery to ethnic minority children and families.* A System of Care for

Children's Mental Health: Expanding the Research Base, Eighth Annual Research Conference Proceedings, March 6-8, Florida Mental Health Institute, Tampa, Florida

Ducheny, K., Alletzhauser, H., Crandell, D., & Schneider, T. (1997). Graduate student professional development. *Professional Psychology: Research and Practice, 28,* 87-91.

Dunn, D. S., & Toedter, L.J. (1991) The collaborative honors project in psychology: Enhancing student and faculty development. *Teaching of Psychology, 18,* 178-180.

Gibson, P.R., Kahn, A.S., & Mathie, V.A. (1996) Undergraduate research groups: Two models. *Teaching Psychology, 23,* 36-38.

Goldman, L. (1979) Research is more than technology. *Counseling Psychologist, 8* (3), 41-44.

Gonzalez, E. (1995) *Connecting the nation: Classrooms, libraries, and health care organizations in the information age.* U.S. Department of Commerce, National Telecommunications and Information Administration (NTIA).

Harris, J. (1998) *Design tools for the Internet-supported classroom.* Association for Supervision and Curriculum Development, Alexandria, VA.

Hollingsworth, P., Johnson, D., & Smith, S. (1998) An evaluation study of interdisciplinary active learning. *Roeper Review, 20* (4), 273-276.

Johnson, D., Johnson, R., & Smith, K. (1991) *Active learning: Cooperation in the college classroom.* Edina, MN: Interaction Books.

Katz, J., & Aspden, P. (1997) *Motivations for and barriers to Internet usage: Results of a national public opinion survey.* Paper presented at the Twenty-fourth Telecommunications Policy Research Conference, Solomons, MD, on October 6, 1996. Morristown, NJ: Bellcore.

Lan, J.J. (1999). *The impact of Internet-based instruction on teacher education: The "paradigm shift."* Paper presented at the Annual Meeting of the American Association of Colleges for Teacher Education (Washington, DC, February 24-27).

Mathew, N.M., Barufaldi, J.P., & Bethel, L.J. (1998) *The effect of electronic networking on preservice elementary teacher's science teaching self-efficacy.* Paper presented at the Annual Meeting of the National Association for Research in Science Teaching (71st, San Diego, CA, April 19-22, 1998).

Miller, F. (1992) Leadership strategies for professional development. *Journal of National Black Nurses Association, 5* (2), 52-59.

Misale, J.M., Gillette, D.H., & del Mas, R.C. (1996) An interdisciplinary, computer-centered approach to active learning. *Teaching of Psychology, 23* (3), 181-184.

McDonald, D.G. (1997) Psychology's surge in undergraduate majors. *Teaching Psychology, 24,* 22-26.

Nixon, M.A. (1998) Collaborative Learning in the Master's of Project Management Distance Learning Degree Program. In: *WebNet 98 World Conference of the WWW, Internet and Intranet Proceedings* (3rd, Orlando, FL, November 7-12).

Ouellette, P. (1999) Moving toward technology-supported instruction in human service practice: The "virtual classroom." *Technology and Human Services, 16* (2/3), 97-111.

Pea, R. (1993) Seeing what we build together: Distributed multimedia learning environments for transformative communications. *The Journal of the Learning Sciences, 3* (3), 285-299.

Pfeiffer, S., & Marmo, P. (1981) The status of training in school psychology and trends toward the future. *Journal of School Psychology, 19* (3), 211-216.

Plante, T. (1998) A laboratory group model for engaging undergraduates in faculty research. *Teaching Psychology, 25,* 128-130.

Schinn, M. (1987) Research by practicing school psychologists: The need for fuel for the lamp. *Professional School Psychology, 2* (4), 235-243.

Shulman, L. (1981) *Identifying, measuring, and teaching helping skills.* New York, NY: Council on Social Work Education.

Skovholt, T.M., & Ronnestad, M.H. (1992). Themes in therapist and counselor development. *Journal of Counseling and Development, 70,* 505-515.

Slavin, R.E. (1991) Synthesis of research on cooperative learning. *Educational Leadership, 48,* 71-82.

Ullrich, M. (1998) Making the Move to On-Line Learning. *In: WebNet 98 World Conference of the WWW, Internet and Intranet Proceedings* (3rd, Orlando, FL, November 7-12).

Wampold, B.E. (1986) Toward quality research in counseling psychology. *Counseling Psychologist*, 14 (1), 37-48

Waugh, M.L., & Ruth, A. (1995) Teleapprenticeships in an elementary science methods class: A description of students' network experience. *Journal of Computers in Mathematics and Science Teaching, 14* (1/2), 77-92.

Wernet, S. P., & Olliges, R. (1998) *The Application of WebCT (Web Course Tools) in social work education.* Conference Proceedings 2nd Annual Information Technology for Social Work Practice and Education, College of Social Work, University of South Carolina, Charleston, SC.

We'd Like to Ask You Some Questions, But We Have to Find You First: An Internet-Based Study of Lesbian Clients in Therapy with Lesbian Feminist Therapists

Georgia K. Quartaro
Terry E. Spier

SUMMARY. This paper explores some issues related to an Internet-based study dealing with lesbian clients' perceptions of their lesbian feminist therapists. A 60-item questionnaire was posted on a Web site so respondents could complete it online, submitting answers anonymously through a forwarding service. Respondents were recruited through postings to 20 listservs that focus on gay/lesbian/bisexual issues or the psychology of women. Data collection proceeded rapidly, with 182 responses within seven weeks. Results indicated that the therapist's sexual and philosophical orientation was important to the client, but that the clients tended to make assumptions about the latter. Specific activities typical of feminist therapy were often missing or were not recollected by clients. The advantages of using the Internet to draw a wide range of respondents is set against the problems of generalizability, the difficulty in communicating

Georgia K. Quartaro, PhD, and Terry E. Spier, MEd, are affiliated with George Brown College, Toronto, Ontario, Canada.

Address correspondence to: Georgia K. Quartaro, PhD, George Brown College, P.O. Box 1015, Station B, Toronto, Ontario, Canada M5T 2T9 (gquartar@ gbrownc.on.ca). A more detailed summary of the study described here is also available on request.

[Haworth co-indexing entry note]: "We'd Like to Ask You Some Questions, But We Have to Find You First: An Internet-Based Study of Lesbian Clients in Therapy with Lesbian Feminist Therapists." Quartaro, Georgia K., and Terry E. Spier. Co-published simultaneously in *Journal of Technology in Human Services* (The Haworth Press, Inc.) Vol. 19, No. 2/3, 2002, pp. 109-118; and: *Using the Internet as a Research Tool for Social Work and Human Services* (ed: Goutham M. Menon) The Haworth Press, Inc., 2002, pp. 109-118. Single or multiple copies of this article are available for a fee from The Haworth Document Delivery Service [1-800-HAWORTH, 9:00 a.m. - 5:00 p.m. (EST). E-mail address: getinfo@haworthpressinc.com].

directly with respondents, and the sample bias inevitable in using self-identified volunteers who have Internet access. *[Article copies available for a fee from The Haworth Document Delivery Service: 1-800-HAWORTH. E-mail address: <getinfo@haworthpressinc.com> Website: <http://www.HaworthPress.com> © 2002 by The Haworth Press, Inc. All rights reserved.]*

KEYWORDS. Feminist therapists, gay and lesbian listserve groups, web-based survey

The potential of the Internet as a medium for survey research is an important adjunct to its role as information transmission and exchange. Identifying and contacting potential research subjects is often a challenge in research design. The convention that university undergraduates constitute an adequate sample from the general population is good evidence of this difficulty. Such conventions are hard to abandon, even though it is obvious that undergraduates do not match the general population on any criterion one might name, because representative or random samples are not easy to draw from large populations. Furthermore, collecting data from widely dispersed respondents often presents additional problems. The Internet provides some unique approaches to addressing these issues.

The less accessible the population of interest, the more difficulties the researcher is likely to encounter in collecting data. These problems have been particularly acute for the researcher who is interested in special or hidden populations, as potential participants can be difficult to contact. Members of these populations do not exist as readily identifiable groups and must usually be located through a sequence of personal and organizational contacts. Hidden populations can be especially challenging to locate, as members must disclose this aspect of their identity. Lesbians are such a population. Non-random samples are standard in research with lesbians because "it is impossible to devise a strategy for reaching a random sample of a hidden population" (Bradford, Ryan, & Rothblum, 1994, p. 231). This paper includes a brief report of a study that used the Internet to collect data from lesbians who have been in therapy with a lesbian feminist therapist.

RESEARCH WITH HIDDEN OR SPECIAL POPULATIONS

The details we describe are from our study of lesbians' experience in therapy, but the issues would be very similar in research with other hidden populations (e.g., saxophone players, stamp collectors, political refugees, illegal immigrants). Samples from populations like these are invariably skewed. They are usually very limited geographically, and many members of the potential sample have no opportunity to participate. The researcher sacrifices representativeness and generalizability in favor of ensuring that the research participants are members of the population of interest.

Additionally, sampling strategies often compromise the anonymity or confidentiality of the research subjects. Subjects may be unwilling to participate or may be less self-disclosing than in a more anonymous research situation. This is especially true if the potential participant thinks there is some risk in self-disclosure, either in general or to this particular researcher. For some, such as the hypothetical saxophone players, this last issue is probably insignificant; for other populations, such as illegal immigrants, it might be paramount. With all such populations, however, the would-be researcher faces the problem of needing to identify the potential participant.

Like members of other hidden populations, lesbians are typically recruited using organizational and personal contacts, convenience or snowball samples, and similar methods. These often restrict the pool of respondents geographically and in other ways. Some large sample sizes have been reported despite these difficulties, particularly when the researcher's only criterion was that the participants self-defined as lesbians. Liddle (1997) reported on a sample of 220 and Morgan (1997) had a sample size of 247. The largest such study (Bradford et al., 1994) was a NIMH-funded survey that reported data from 1,925 lesbian respondents recruited through newsletters, community organizations, and personal networks. In contrast, however, most of the research with lesbians draws on small, local samples or rests on clinical and anecdotal reports.

It was evident that the participants we were interested in contacting were going to be difficult to find. Previous research indicated that most lesbians preferred to work with a lesbian therapist and that a high proportion of lesbians had been in therapy. Nevertheless, locating a reasonable number of potential participants through networks or advertising would have been difficult and time-consuming. Guaranteeing anonymity was complicated, which might affect respondents' willingness to disclose. One of the researchers was also active as a therapist in this community and would be known to some potential participants, either personally or by reputation. Above all, we wanted to draw responses from a wider range of participants. While the nature of the research precluded random sampling and generalizability, we wanted to reach beyond one city (Toronto, Canada), one community of respondents, and their experiences with a relatively small number of lesbian feminist therapists. We wanted to contact clients from a broader range of settings and ask about their experiences with their therapists.

FEATURES OF INTERNET-BASED RESEARCH

"The Internet is as much a collection of communities as a collection of technologies, and its success is largely attributable to both satisfying basic community needs as well as utilizing the community . . . to push the infrastructure forward" (Leiner et al., 1999). The proliferation of websites, discussion groups, and electronic mailing lists (e.g., LISTSERV) on the Internet has created connections that enable people who have interests, experiences, affinities, or aspects of identity in common to communicate without regard to geographical boundaries. Subscribers to electronic mailing lists share information and often develop relationships through exchanges shared by all subscribers. Through the Internet, people can transcend many differences to focus on the topic or interest that joins them. This form of community allows people to be highly self-disclosing about some aspects of themselves while retaining as much control as they wish over identifying information.

This development creates some interesting opportunities and challenges for the researcher whose investigation centers on a population that is not easy to access directly. Information about the research and invitations to participate can be made available to people who have already identified themselves to one another as members of the population of interest. If the research invitation is posted on a list or discussion group, members of this special population will see it, and, as in our study, members of subgroups within that population will learn about it. Subjects can participate in the research without revealing their identity or even having any direct contact with the researcher. The near-global reach of such lists and discussion groups makes it possible to get a reasonable number of respondents even from small or highly dispersed special populations.

There are still limitations to such samples. The Internet is not equally available to all, even within North America and Northern Europe, and certainly not worldwide. Further, many members of any potential special population who have e-mail and Internet access may not be affiliated with these discussion groups or lists. Respondents will probably be biased toward those who have a stronger affiliation with the population and are more interested in exchanges with other members of that community. People who prefer to get information in person or through books and magazines may be underrepresented, as may those who are less comfortable with or have less access to electronic media. This probably introduces systematic biases of education, socioeconomic status, and age. Our demographic data reflects some of these biases. The characteristics and biases typical of volunteer samples can also be expected.

The process of collecting data can be greatly facilitated using the Internet. If appropriate participants are contacted and volunteer, data can be collected very quickly. The participant who decides to complete the research instrument is likely to do so very soon after reading the posting. As soon as the survey is completed, it is submitted electronically. There is no waiting for the respondent to finish writing answers, find the envelope, and remember to mail it. If the structure of the survey permits computer-based analysis, this phase of the research can proceed very quickly as well. The data arrive already formatted and are easy to add to the analysis.

DESCRIPTION OF THE STUDY

Our study focused on the experience of lesbians in therapy with lesbian feminist therapists. Previous research in this area consisted of surveys on the preferences of lesbians for a lesbian therapist (e.g., Bradford et al., 1994; Morgan, 1997). There were also theoretical papers, clinical accounts, and anecdotal reports (e.g., Brown, 1989; Burstow, 1992; Elise, 1991; Gartrell, 1985, 1992) about the benefits to the client of matching the therapist's and client's sexual orientation. However, research that tapped the clients' perceptions about specific experiences of therapy was limited to unidimensional satisfaction ratings (e.g., Liddle, 1997). Similarly, writers (e.g., Bustow, 1992; Gartrell, 1985) assumed that lesbian clients would choose feminist therapists, because this political and philosophical position would be most congruent with the clients' own. However, there was no research on the clients' experience of feminist therapy.

The study explored three general areas. How did the client experience working with a lesbian therapist? How did the client experience working with a feminist therapist? What perceptions and recollections did the client have about specific actions and interventions that should be characteristic of feminist therapy? We wanted a finer-grained depiction of the clients' experience, beyond a simple expression of satisfaction or preference and from the clients' perspective, which we could compare with the clinical accounts written by therapists.

Method

In designing this study, the challenge of identifying potential respondents quickly became apparent. In effect, potential respondents had to be members of two hidden populations, lesbians and psychotherapy clients. The Internet provided an opportunity to reach a wide pool of potential respondents. A call for participants, including a study description and the criteria, was posted on about 20 electronic mailing lists and discussion groups focused on lesbians, gay/lesbian/bisexual psychology, and women interested in psychology. Subscribers were also asked to forward the posting to other suitable lists. This was an attempt to broaden the pool of participants and to reach beyond North America, as the international lists used still had a strong geographical bias.

Potential participants were directed to a website that gave further information about the study, the criteria for participation, a consent letter, and the questionnaire itself. Those who wished to respond could complete a closed answer, 60-item questionnaire online and submit it immediately. Responses were returned to one of the researchers (T. S.) through an e-mail forwarding service that deleted the respondent's e-mail address. This guaranteed anonymity. Respondents were invited to contact one of the researchers by e-mail if they had questions or comments, and about a dozen did so. They were also able to request a summary of the findings. This correspondence was completely separate from the response to the questionnaire and the two could not be linked in any way. Potential respondents who did not have convenient Internet access or were not comfortable using it could send an e-mail request for a printed copy of the questionnaire and about 10% of the returns were in this format.

The questionnaire posed a series of questions about the respondent's experience in individual therapy with a lesbian feminist therapist. Respondents were asked about their choices when they began therapy, the importance of the therapist's sexual and philosophical orientation, ways the therapist dealt with some specific issues, and overall satisfaction. The questionnaire also included 13 demographic items.

Characteristics of the Respondents

Completed questionnaires were returned by 182 respondents. Although locating respondents over the Internet was done to broaden the range of respondents, the vast majority were white (89%), North American (89%) and urban (56% lived in cities, 19% in suburbs). Education was generally high, with 85% having at least one university degree. In age, most respondents were 30-39 (36%) or 40-49 (31%) and only 3% were over 60. Income and social class were more varied. Though 20% earned less than $12,501 per year, only 4% described themselves as "living in poverty." Just over half (55%) described themselves as "middle class," and a personal annual income of $25,001-$50,000 (U. S.) was reported by 41%. Despite the consistency of the sample, the respondents were more varied as a result of recruiting via the Internet than they would have been by any other means available. These socioeconomic characteristics are similar to those reported in other studies. They are probably an approximate reflection of the demographics of lesbians who have been in individual psychotherapy and who currently have access to the Internet, at least in the U. S. and Canada.

Rate of Data Collection

Data collection proceeded very rapidly. Within two weeks of the postings, 115 responses were received. A second request to each of the lists resulted in 15 more responses by the fourth week of data collection. (In contrast, only 5 of 50 mailed questionnaires had been returned by this point.) The original intention had been to collect about 100 responses. However, seven weeks of data collection resulted in 182 completed questionnaires. We can imagine no other method that would result in such a large response so quickly and at so little cost.

Key Results

In general, respondents reported high satisfaction with therapy. Most respondents reported that they had deliberately sought a therapist who was both lesbian (76%) and feminist (66%). Respondents were more diligent in determining that the therapist was a lesbian, however, with 37% reporting that they assumed the therapist was a feminist although this was never stated directly. Overall, the therapist's sexual orientation seemed more important to the clients, with 93% agreeing that they expected the therapist to understand their experience as a lesbian and even more saying that there were some things the therapist understood without needing explanation (96%). Thus, most respondents deliberately chose a lesbian therapist and believed that she understood their experience implicitly. However, only 1/3 thought that the therapist worked differently than she would with a heterosexual client and even fewer stated that this was important to them.

Reports of the therapists' behavior and interventions were similarly surprising. With the exception of therapist self-disclosure, practices that are characteristic of feminist therapy apparently were absent in many instances. For example, discussions of power relationships or of the sociopolitical context of the client's problems were reported much less often than the clinical literature would suggest. Of course, as this is the client's recollection, it may be that the client did not notice or did not accurately remember the therapist's actions. In any event, it is clear that the clients' perceptions and judgments about their experience in therapy are more complex than the previous research on preference and satisfaction alone would suggest.

ISSUES IN INTERNET-BASED SURVEY RESEARCH

Several issues arise out of our use of the Internet to gather data. The anonymity afforded to respondents also means that the researcher cannot be certain that respondents actually meet the criteria established for the study. In our case, we cannot say with absolute certainty that the respondents had been in therapy with lesbian feminist therapists, that they were lesbians, or even that they were women. Given the circumscribed nature of the lists on which the request for participation was posted, all or almost all of the responses were probably bona fide. Only subscribers to the lists could access the postings, and the material that circulates among subscribers is of little interest to the general reader. Nevertheless, the advantage of offering anonymity to respondents is offset, at least in part, by a corresponding reliance on the respondents to honor the criteria the researchers have established. This issue is not unique to this study. By its nature, the Internet facilitates protection and control of identifying personal information as well as its distortion or falsification. While this issue can occur for any study that involves anonymity, the distance the Internet places between subject and researcher increases this risk.

Linking the researcher and participant electronically also removes some of the casual contact between them. In many studies, the researcher's observations or a participant's offhand remark sparks further thinking and adds to the researcher's understanding. Like a large-scale mail survey, the Internet precluded that possibility in this design. We were totally reliant on two pilot subjects for reactions to questions, timing, etc. Although it is possible to have dialogue with the participants or to offer clarification by e-mail, in practice this is relatively cumbersome and unlikely to occur. This aspect of Internet-based data collection might proceed quite differently if the researcher uses a free-response instrument. The apparent informality and intimacy of Internet communication may well lead respondents to be more self-revealing than they would in a more conventional interview setting. The capture of data in text form (as opposed to field notes or taped interviews) would facilitate qualitative analysis and reduce the tedious, time-consuming nature of this research.

Opportunities to participate in Internet-based research are increasing rapidly. Consumer research panels on the Internet are in their infancy but are proliferating. At present, these panels ask potential members for some general information about themselves. In the future, this pool of information will probably expand, creating direct access to members of special populations who are willing to participate in research. This is a logical development from the increasingly-refined Internet consumer profiles being developed by advertisers. Researchers should be able to draw on large (if not necessarily representative) samples of populations that are even more difficult to access than the one in this study. At present, these panels range from fairly serious research enterprises that resemble other consumer or political polls to do-it-yourself survey sites that invite respondents' curiosity about almost any question.

Widespread surveying across the Internet may also affect subjects' expectations and willingness to participate. In our research, moderators of a few lists were wary and expressed concerns about exploitation, stating that in the past some researchers had used the list to collect data without any genuine interest in the subscribers' own purpose and priorities for the list. Broadcast postings can be interpreted as "spam." Public skepticism, like the reactions to deception in social psychology experiments, may come to limit the usefulness of the Internet for data collection.

Finally, the use of the Internet for data collection ties directly to its use for other kinds of research. In the course of doing this project, there were e-mail discussions and exchanges with researchers elsewhere in Canada, in several U. S. states, and on other continents. These researchers commented on our questionnaire content and design, identified or asked about resource material, and shared their experiences, including sending information and results of an unpublished Australian study somewhat similar to ours. This would not have occurred in a conventional local study. The Internet makes it relatively easy for people who are interested in the same topic to find one another, even if they are not well-known, and to discuss methodological issues. Further strategies and refinements for Internet-based research will continue to emerge from these dialogues.

REFERENCES

Bradford, J., Ryan, C. & Rothblum, E. (1994). National lesbian health care survey: Implications for mental health care. *Journal of Consulting and Clinical Psychology, 62* (2), 228-242.

Brown, L. (1989). Beyond thou shalt not: Thinking about ethics in the lesbian therapy community. In Esther Rothblum & Ellen Cole (Eds.). *Loving boldly: Issues facing lesbians* (pp. 13-25). New York: Harrington Park Press.

Burstow, B. (1992). *Radical feminist therapy: Working in the context of violence.* Newbury Park, CA: Sage Publishing.

Elise, D. (1991). When sexual and romantic feelings permeate the therapeutic relationship. In C. Silverstein (Ed.). *Gays, lesbians and their therapists: Studies in psychotherapy* (pp. 52067). New York: W. W. Norton & Company.

Gartrell, N. (1985). Issues in psychotherapy with lesbian women. *The Stone Center for Developmental Services and Studies,* No. 83-04. Work in Progress. Boston: Wellesley College.

Gartrell, N. (1992). Boundaries in lesbian therapy relationships. *Women & Therapy, 12* (3), 29-50.

Leiner, B. M., Cerf, V. G., Clark, D. D., Kahn, R. E., Kleinrock, L., Lynch, D. C., Postel, J., Roberts, L. G. & Wolff, S. (1999). *A brief history of the Internet. Internet Society (ISOC).* [Online]. Available: http://www.isoc.org/internet/history/brief.html

Liddle, B. J. (1997). Gay and lesbian clients' selection of therapists and utilization of therapy. *Psychotherapy, 34* (1), 11-18.

Morgan, K. S. (1997). Why lesbians choose therapy: Presenting problems, attitudes, and political concerns. *Journal of Gay & Lesbian Social Services, 6* (3), 57-75.

Problems and Promises in the Study of Virtual Communities

Susan C. Kinnevy
Guy Enosh

SUMMARY. This paper discusses several methodological approaches to the study of virtual communities, including comparative designs, statistical approaches, and ethnography. In particular, we present results from one study that exemplifies both the problems and promises inherent in researching virtual communities. This study examines the daily interactions of peace activists in a virtual community devoted to nonviolent solutions to world problems. By analyzing narrative messages exchanged over a four-month period categorically in terms of topic, type, scope, and content, the study explores community design issues of gatekeeping and normative standards in a virtual community.   *[Article copies available for a fee from The Haworth Document Delivery Service: 1-800-HAWORTH. E-mail address: <getinfo@haworthpressinc.com> Website: <http://www.HaworthPress.com> © 2002 by The Haworth Press, Inc. All rights reserved.]*

KEYWORDS. Virtual communities, community design, peace activism, research methods, ethnography

---

Susan C. Kinnevy, MSW, is affiliated with the University of Pennsylvania, School of Social Work, Center for the Study of Youth Policy, 4200 Pine Street, 3rd Floor, Philadelphia, PA 19104 (kinnevy@ssw.upenn.edu).

Guy Enosh, MSW, PhD, is Lecturer, School of Social Work, University of Haifa, Mt. Carmel, Haifa 31905, Israel (enosh@ssw.upenn.edu).

[Haworth co-indexing entry note]: "Problems and Promises in the Study of Virtual Communities." Kinnevy, Susan C., and Guy Enosh. Co-published simultaneously in *Journal of Technology in Human Services* (The Haworth Press, Inc.) Vol. 19, No. 2/3, 2002, pp. 119-134; and: *Using the Internet as a Research Tool for Social Work and Human Services* (ed: Goutham M. Menon) The Haworth Press, Inc., 2002, pp. 119-134. Single or multiple copies of this article are available for a fee from The Haworth Document Delivery Service [1-800-HAWORTH, 9:00 a.m. - 5:00 p.m. (EST). E-mail address: getinfo@haworthpressinc.com].

This paper discusses several methodological approaches to the study of virtual communities, including comparative designs, statistical approaches, and ethnography. In particular, we present results from one study that exemplifies both the problems and promises inherent in researching virtual communities. This study examines the daily interactions of peace activists in a virtual community devoted to nuclear disarmament and non-violent solutions to world problems. By analyzing narrative messages exchanged over a four-month period categorically in terms of topic, type, and scope, as well as by the presence or absence of personal content and conflictual-tone in the messages, the study explores community design issues of gatekeeping and normative standards in a virtual community.

BACKGROUND AND SIGNIFICANCE

Virtual communities are constructed through communication and interaction that occurs instantaneously on several levels and through several dimensions: e-mail, listservs, web pages and hyperlinks. In face-to-face communication there is an inherent expectation that an immediate response will follow an initiated communication. But in virtual communities, participants have a choice as to the timing of both sending and receiving communications. The scientific study of virtual communities, while holding great promise for researchers to understand the ramifications of electronic technology on social interaction, also faces problems not previously encountered in the study of face-to-face communities.

Research on Internet communication and community-building ranges from theoretical discussions on the nature of artificial vs. human intelligence through policy discussions on legal issues of ownership and appropriate content to analytic discussions of e-mail exchanges, webpages and usenet groups (Heim, 1993; Hill & Hughes, 1998; Plant, 1997; Wooley, 1992). But research that moves from theory to analysis of existing virtual communities is rare. As with any other study of communication, analysis of virtual communities consists of freezing a section of time to explore what is essentially part of an ongoing process. But the fluidity of the medium necessitates a rethinking of our approach to research. As social scientists, we are accustomed to doing research from a linear perspective, which assumes that one event follows another in a more or less continuous fashion. However, Internet technology and cyberspace enable non-linear communication. Cyber communities that are linked non-linearly both in time and space are rapidly creating a new ecological niche that requires creativity in applying traditional research methodologies.

METHODOLOGICAL APPROACHES FOR THE STUDY OF VIRTUAL COMMUNITIES

Most published research on virtual communities has used qualitative approaches, drawing mostly from ethnography, conversation analysis (CA) or discourse analysis (DA) (e.g., Coe, 1998; Downey, Dumit, & Williams, 1995; Escobar, 1994; Fox & Roberts, 1999; Rice & Love, 1987). The use of DA and CA approaches is particularly useful in capturing the flow of communication and interaction between members of a virtual community, since such communities are by their nature discursive communities.[1] Discourse analysis enables the researcher to reconstruct the interpersonal interactions and the processes by which meanings are constructed. It also allows exploration of the influence of the forms of communication on the content of the communication. For example, asking a question and not getting an immediate response may be perceived as an insult leading to an escalation of conflict in the interpersonal communication.

As interesting as these qualitative approaches are, there is a paucity of quantitatively based research on virtual communities and a lack of integrated (quantitative and qualitative) approaches. Developing applications of quantitative approaches could take several possible routes. The most basic one would be to use content analysis in order to quantify various levels (forms) in which communication takes place, as well as to quantify the substance of the communications. One level might be a posting to a listserv that is then posted to other listserves, thus expanding the definition of what is the referent community (Kang & Choi, 1999). The posting may be forwarded from another communication source (a personal e-mail, another listserv, web site, media communication, etc.). The listserv itself may be monitored by the owner, regulating the types of postings and their contents, or may be open. All these issues impact on the type and content of communications within a listserv and through that, impact the normative boundaries of the virtual community and its instrumental goals. Thus, content analysis should not be limited to the actual content of the messages, but should examine the process by which the form of inputs influences both the content and the rules by which communications happen. Furthermore, the relative influence of individuals within a discursive community may be the result of the relative status and power they hold in that community, the amount of inputs or level of involvement in that community, and the content of the messages they send.

In order to examine all these variables, quantitative content analysis is a first and necessary step. Nevertheless, content analysis can be performed only after an ethnographic observation of or involvement with the cyber community (Downey, Dumit, & Williams, 1995; Escobar, 1994). Without such immersion in the processes and life of the community, the researcher runs the risk of imposing a barren and preconceived frame of analysis that has little to do with the specific field of study. This type of immersion is common in ethnographic studies of face-to-face communities and is both easier and harder to accomplish in virtual communities. Unlike face-to-face communities, virtual communities can be observed unobtrusively; they can also be observed at the researcher's convenience since the communications can remain in place indefinitely or can be archived by the researcher. On the other hand, virtual communities do not offer the researcher the opportunity to observe non-verbal communications, e.g., hand gestures, body language, and facial expressions, which often have a real impact on community processes.

Following the ethnographic observation and collection of data, e.g., e-mail messages, the next step would be analyzing the data in order to construct a coherent coding scheme for categories that represent the major content areas and forms of the communications. After deciding on the categories relevant for the study of a specific community, operationalizing the coding scheme, and coding the contents and forms of communication, the researcher may move on to various analytic approaches. The next logical step would be to get a further "feel" for the data by examining the distribution of the various categories. From this point on, the study can be carried out focusing on each participant's contribution to the communication.

Another way to approach the data would be to look at the interaction between individuals and the link between individual (micro) level communications and group (macro) level outcomes and processes, using time-lagged approaches such as event history analysis (e.g., Allison, 1995) or aggregated time-series analysis (e.g., Ostrom, 1990). Such longitudinal approaches would enable the examination of the impact of an individual's communication patterns on the communication patterns of other individuals, and the outcomes for the entire virtual community. Such approaches depend on having a comprehensive systemic theory that enables the researchers to conceptualize a clear and comprehensive coding of the various levels of communication (the message content level, the individual participant level, and the community level processes and outcomes).

ETHNOGRAPHIC CASE STUDY

Virtual communities, which are exclusively voluntary associations, deal with at least some of the same issues as face-to-face communities, e.g., gatekeeping, and normative value construction. Virtual communities, however, often rely on a moderator to set and maintain boundaries, reduce conflict, and control the flow of discourse. In the following participant-observation study of 246 listserv messages in a peace activist virtual community, a naturally occurring change from a monitored to an unmonitored list elicited the following research questions: (1) What is the impact of list monitoring on the topic, type, scope, and content of community participation? (2) What is the impact of list monitoring on the emergence of individual voices? Another interesting question would be the comparison of the impact of different list monitors of the same type of communities. However, such a comparison would require collecting data on at least one other virtual peace activist community and is therefore beyond the scope of this study.

METHODS

Design. This study was ethnographic, consisting of non-participant observation of e-mail messages from a virtual peace activist community over a four-month period from mid-December, 1998 through mid-April, 1999. The first author informed the list owner that she would be observing the list for research purposes. A major change in the community occurred at the beginning of April when the list moved from being monitored by one individual to being a non-monitored, direct-post listserv. This change afforded the authors an opportunity to evaluate a naturally occurring pre-post situation.

Population.[2] A total of 246 messages were observed. Duplicate messages were removed, resulting in a final population of 241 messages (139 messages from the monitored list period and 102 messages from the non-monitored list period).

Coding Framework. Messages were coded into a quantitative dataset that tracked the messages by topic (10), type (10), geographic range or scope (4), origin (11), and content (presence or absence of personal content and conflictual-tone). Table 1 represents the coding scheme for the analysis of the data.

Research questions were answered using the following categorical analysis: (1) Content of communication was analyzed through the categories of topic and presence or absence of personal content and conflictual-tone; and (2) Form of communication was analyzed through the categories of type and scope.

RESULTS

The following analysis examines 241 e-mail messages, both as a whole and from a pre-post monitored list perspective. As Table 2 indicates, the study covered a period of 127 days, only 20 of which were unmonitored. There were 47 days with no messages posted, but 45 of those were during the monitored list period. In other words, 42% of the total monitored days carried no messages, as opposed to 10% of the unmonitored days. Similarly, the longest period of consecutive days without messages was 7 (7%) in the monitored list period, as opposed to 1 day (5%) during the non-monitored period. Although the total number of messages (monitored = 142, unmonitored = 104) was 246, there were 5 duplicate messages, bringing the sample total to 241 (monitored = 139, unmonitored = 102). The highest number of messages posted on a given day went from 7 during the monitored phase to 18 during the non-monitored phase; the average number of messages went from 1.3 to 5.2.

As indicated in Figure 1, the topic that garnered the largest share of messages (n = 73) over the course of the study was the war in Kosovo. Subsequent analysis revealed that 58.9% of the Kosovo messages generated messages with a conflictual-tone, as opposed to only 5.4% of the messages regarding the bombing of Iraq (n = 37). Kosovo messages also differed from the combined Iraq/Political Prisoners messages with regard to personal content. Over 50% of the Kosovo messages registered high on personal content, as opposed to 33.7% on the Iraq/Political Prisoner messages (n = 76).

Regarding changes in the type of message pre-and post list change, Figure 2 reveals that the unmonitored list decreased the number of analyses and announcements posted, but increased the level of personal

TABLE 1. Coding Framework

TOPICS	TYPES	SCOPE	ORIGIN	CONTENT
Iraq	Analysis	International	List Owner, during moderated period (LO)	Personal Content
Kosovo	Announcement	National	Original List Owner, during unmoderated period (LO2)	Conflictual Tone
Political Prisoners & Trials	News Article	Regional	Director of State Chapter of the Peace Activist Group (DSC)	
Bill Clinton	Personal Comment	Local	National Parent Organization of the Group (NP)	
Media Coverage	Press Release		Another International Activist Group (IA)	
Disarmament & Defense Spending	Media Event		Community Members with regular and numerous contributions (CM1, CM2, and CM3)	
Generic Protests	Protest Action Alert		New Community Member during unmoderated period (CM4)	
Information about the List	Other Protest Information		Others	
Democracy	Response to Other Messages			
Miscellaneous	Miscellaneous			

comment and responses to other messages. Figure 3 shows the scope of the messages changing from a very local and national focus to a regional and international focus. Figure 4 indicates that as messages from the list owner (LO) disappeared after the change to an unmonitored list, the individual member who was the original list owner (LO2) emerged just as strongly after the change, although in a member rather than owner capacity. DSC, who participated moderately before the change, ranked as the highest individual participant after the change. The role of the national parent organization (NP) decreased dramatically after the change, along with the role of the international organization (IA). Since the international focus increased after the change, it seems odd that the role of the international organization decreased, leaving the reason for the changes open for speculation. While the role of one individual member (CM1) decreased after the change, two other individual members

TABLE 2. Pre- and Post-List Change Comparison

	MONITORED	UNMONITORED
Number of days in the study	107	20
Number of days with no messages	45 (42%)	2 (10%)
Consecutive days with no messages	7 (7%)	1 (5%)
Total messages posted	142	104
Number of duplicate messages	3	2
Total messages in sample	139	102
Highest number of messages in one day	7	18
Average number of messages in one day	1.33	5.2

FIGURE 1. Change in Topic of Messages

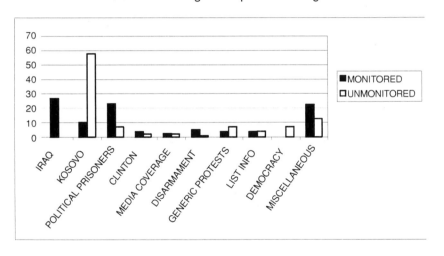

(CM2 and CM3) increased their participation and a new member (CM4) also became vocal after the change. Regarding the content of the messages, Figure 5 displays an increase in messages with a conflictual-tone and is accompanied by a decrease in messages with personal content.

After examining the changes in the distribution of categories that resulted from a change in the monitoring status of the list, the authors estimated logistic regression models, examining the role of personal voices in the community, the impact of the topic, type, and scope of message and the impact of list monitoring on those personal voices. All models used the dummy variable coding with absence (0) as the refer-

FIGURE 2. Change in Type of Message

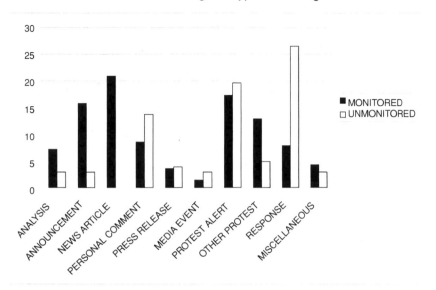

FIGURE 3. Change in Scope of Messages

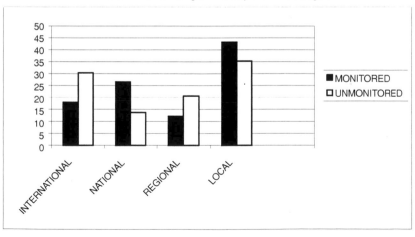

FIGURE 4. Change in Origin of Messages

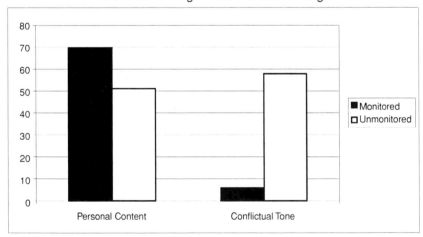

FIGURE 5. Change in Content of Message

ence (omitted) category. Two dependent variables were used– "personal" and "conflict" representing the probability of including personal experiences/content and conflictual-tone in a message to the list. The results are presented in Tables 3 and 4 respectively. A methodological note is necessary here. As discussed previously, the population the authors examine is the entire message population for the time period in question. Significance levels for the regression coefficients are meaningful only

TABLE 3. Logistic Regression–Personal

Variable Ctg	Variable	Model A (Odds Ratio)[1]	Model B (Odds Ratio)	Model C (Odds Ratio)
Original	LO2	1.10	0.46	0.53
(Participant)	SD	1.84	1.4	1.5
	NP	0.23**	0.22**	0.20**
	IA	0.08***	0.04***	0.04***
	CM1	2.75	3.47	3.17
	CM2	1.1	1.00	1.09
	CM4	2.2	1.52	1.96
	CM3	1.1	0.62	0.60
	LO (owner)	0.72	0.75	0.68
Topic	Iraq	--	1.27	1.13
	Kosovo	--	1.22	1.36
	Prisoners	--	2.66*	2.60*
Type	News article	--	0.48 ^{V}	0.49 ^{V}
	Alert	--	0.71	0.76
	Response	--	1.08	1.20
Scope	International	--	0.88	0.88
	National	--	0.38 ^{V}	0.36 ^{V}
	Local	--	0.54	0.52
Conflict	Conflictual-tone	--	5.20***	5.90***
Monitoring Status	Monitored	--	--	1.58
	Constant (B)	0.5960	0.7960	0.4896
	−2LL (df)	287.982 (9)	260.192 (19)	259.188 (20)

^{V} $p < 0.1$; *$p < 0.05$; **$p < 0.01$; ***$p < 0.001$
[1] Odds Ratio is the exponent coefficient [exp(B)], and may be interpreted as the increase in the odds-ratio for the inclusion of personal content in a message for each unit increase in the independent variable, controlling for all other variables in the models. Values lower than 1.0 *lower* the odds-ratio.

when dealing with a representative sample. From a technical perspective those significance levels should be ignored. However, they can be regarded as indicating the relative explanatory power of certain variables, while controlling for all other variables in the model. Accordingly, the presentation of results will show the results for all the variables in each model. However, due to space considerations, the discussion of the relative impact of each variable will focus only on those that show some level of "significance" (at least $p < 0.1$ level).

TABLE 4. Logistic Regression: Conflictual-Tone of Messages

Variable Ctg	Variable	Model A (OR)[1]	Model B (OR)	Model C (OR)
Origin	LO2	8.68***	6.64**	3.86^V
(Participant)	SD	2.68*	1.81	1.80
	NP	0.60	1.38	2.79
	IA	1.58	4.88	15.24*
	CM1	0.32	0.19	0.37
	CM2	0.43	0.17	0.16
	CM4	5.20 ^{V}	2.22	1.09
	CM3	3.47	5.22	6.35
	LO (owner)	0.00	0.00	0.00
Topic	Iraq	--	0.41	1.06
	Kosovo	--	4.89**	2.78*
	Prisoners	--	0.00	0.00
Type	News article	--	4.23**	4.97*
	Alert	--	1.04	0.98
	Response	--	7.23**	4.74*
Scope	International	--	0.28 ^{V}	0.26
	National	--	0.42	0.69
	Local	--	0.39	0.44
Personal	Personal content	--	5.32***	6.52***
Monitoring Status	Monitored	--	--	0.08***
	Constant (B)	−1.2443	−2.5467	−1.7132
	−2LL (df)	235.836 (9)	154.400 (19)	135.336 (20)

^{V} $p < 0.1$; *$p < 0.05$; **$p < .01$; ***$p < 0.001$
[1] OR (Odds Ratio) is the exponent coefficient [exp(B)], and may be interpreted as the increase in the odds-ratio for the inclusion of personal content in a message for each unit increase in the independent variable, controlling for all other variables in the models. Values lower than 1.0 *lower* the odds-ratio.

Table 3, which examines the impact of the variables on personal content in the messages, displays three nested models. Model A compares the odds of a message containing personal content among the major contributors to the list. Model B adds to this analysis the odds of various topics, types, scopes, and conflictual-tone impacting on the personal content of the messages. Model C controls for the monitoring status of the list (pre- and-post list change).

Model B represents a significant improvement in explanatory power when compared to Model A (Chi-square difference between the −2LL values of the models is 27.8, with 10 df, p < 0.01). Model C does not exhibit more explanatory power than model B (Chi-square difference is 1.04, 1 df). This lack of significance indicates that monitoring status did not impact on the inclusion of personal content in the messages.

Focusing on Model A, two participants (NP, the national parent organization, and IA, an international peace organization) emerge as negatively related to personal content. Model B, in which the topics, types of messages, scope and conflictual content were added to the analysis, shows that the topic of "political prisoners" has a significant impact on personal content, as well as the use of conflictual-tone in the message. More specifically, the odds for a message including personal content coming from NP are about 1 to 5, and for IA are about 1 to 25. However, some other categories seem to impact on the inclusion of personal content. Of the topics, the issue of prisoners had an odds ratio of 2.6 to elicit personal content, messages related to national scope tended to lower the odds-ratio, while the use of conflictual-tone raised the odds for inclusion of personal content to more than 5 to 1.

Table 4 examines the impact of the same set of variables on the odds for having a conflictual-tone in the message. Comparing the three models, we can see that each is a significant improvement from the previous model. The difference in $-2LL$ between Model B and Model C is 81.4 with 10 df, and between Model B and Model C is about 19, with 1 df. The increased significance in the shift from Model B to Model C is related to the change in the monitoring of the list. This change may also be deduced from the high level of significance registered for the "Monitoring Status" coefficient, which serves as a control variable and shows that the odds for having conflictual-tone in a message have increased by a 12.5 odds-ratio shifting from monitored to non-monitored list.

Model A shows three voices as significantly carrying conflictual messages: LO2, DSC and CM4. However, the level of significance drops when we include in Model C the other variables and the relative conflictual-tone of IA emerges as substantially strong. Controlling for all other variables, the odds-ratio for a conflictual message from this organization is about 15 to 1. The topic of Kosovo was directly related to conflictual content with odds-ratio of almost 3; the messages including new articles had an odds-ratio for conflictual content of almost 5; and messages including personal content have an odds-ratio for having also a conflictual-tone of more than 6 to 1.

DISCUSSION

The first research question addressed by this study asked about the impact of list monitoring on four components of communication: topic, type, scope, and content (presence of absence of personal content and conflictual tone). Analysis revealed that topic and content are interwoven in a way that calls for a discussion of their impact as interactive. The same is true of the interaction between type and scope of messages.

Topic and Content of Messages. The frequency findings regarding conflictual-tone in the Kosovo messages seem to indicate that Kosovo was inherently a more conflictual topic than Iraq and one that elicited more of a personal emotional response. In addition, the U. S. intervention in Kosovo coincided almost precisely with the opening up of the listserv, further confounding the possibility of determining the impact of the list change versus the impact of Kosovo as a topic. However, the regression analysis also demonstrates a strong relationship to the topic of Kosovo and the presence of a conflictual-tone. The analysis further shows the impact of five other variables on conflictual-tone while controlling for the impact of Kosovo as a topic. The stronger impact here seems to be the effect of the change in monitoring status of the list. Thus, though the Kosovo issue contributed significantly to the emergence of conflictual-tones in messages, it does seems that monitoring the list suppressed inputs with conflictual-tones.

Regardless of the cause of the change in conflictual-tone, pre- and post-the list change, it is important to note the kind of conflict that emerged in discussions of Kosovo. Whereas Iraq occasioned no real questioning of community pacifist norms, Kosovo elicited active debate about pacifist ideology and the limits of non-violence as a means of protest. For the first time, community members created a public forum that resembled an electronic town hall meeting. The result, while certainly not a complete normative change in values, is still notable in that a subtle shift in norms seemed to make allowances for gray areas on the ideological front.

Type and Scope of Messages. The change in type of message from analyses and announcements to personal comment and responses to other messages may reflect a reaction to the topic of Kosovo dominating the unmonitored list. The reasons for the change from a local and national scope to a regional and international scope are difficult to analyze. Since there are actually fewer messages from either the national parent organization or the international organization after the list change, it is possible to speculate that the increase in international scope stems from the fact that more individuals from other countries began to contribute after the change. The increase in regional messages almost surely reflects the increase in participation of DSC, an individual member who lives in a different region than LO2, the original gatekeeper.

Emerging Individual Voices. The second research question asked about the impact of list monitoring on the emergence of individual voices. The disappearance of owner-originated messages from LO after the list change was expected, but the interesting development was the emergence of LO2 as an individual voice. On an observational level, the authors noted a change in the tone and content of LO2's messages after he lost his official gatekeeping role. He seemed to become more stri-dent, even somewhat petulant, leading the authors to believe he was having a hard time giving up his ownership of the list. On the other hand, DSC became quite eloquent in the tone of his messages, particu-larly with regard to his spiritual beliefs and their relationship to his ideo-logical commitment to pacifism.

In his original capacity as gatekeeper, LO's voice was authoritative and businesslike; he seemed to view his duties primarily as functional, concentrating on the transmission of information. Because DSC became so outspoken and passionate in his communications after the list change, his voice began to dominate the list and seemed to liberate other voices, as indicated by the increase in messages from two other members and the participation of one new member. DSC became the emotional center of the list and its de facto gatekeeper, even though LO2 continued to partici-pate heavily. The change in gatekeeping also reflected a change in more fluid norms. This study is exploratory and many avenues remain unex-amined. The methodological design may prove capable of producing more rigorous results in subsequent applications.

CONCLUSION

The purpose of this article was twofold: (1) to delineate methodological issues that arise in the study of virtual communities, and suggest a compre-hensive research strategy, combining qualitative and quantitative ap-proaches; and (2) to partially demonstrate the use of such a strategy through an exploratory case study of a specific virtual community. The dis-cussion of methodological approaches to the study of virtual communities spanned various qualitative approaches that might be used to study virtual communities, and elaborated on the possible integration of qualitative and quantitative approaches in this field. Furthermore, the discussion empha-sized the needed bridge between individual (micro) level analysis and group (macro) level analysis. The examination of the ethnographic study was presented in order to illustrate the way in which those methodologies might be combined and applied to a concrete case study. This exemplification by no means exhausts the universe of possible integration of qualitative and quantitative methodologies in the study of virtual communities. Although analysis of such a malleable medium is daunting at first, more exploration of methodological approaches is encouraged because virtual communities are seemingly the wave of the future.

NOTES

1. Discursive communities refer to communities that are defined by their communication, e.g., self-help support groups, informal gossip networks, etc.

2. Since all messages for a given time period were used in the study, the n = 246 represents the entire population of messages rather than a sample of messages.

REFERENCES

Allison, P. D. (1995). *Survival analysis using the SAS system: A practical guide.* Cary, NC: SAS Institute Inc.

Downey, G. L., Dumit, J., & Williams, S. (1995). Cyborg anthropology. *Cultural Anthropology, 10,* 264-269.

Escobar, A. (1994). Welcome to Cyberia: Notes on the anthropology of cyberculture. *Current Anthropology, 35,* 211-232.

Fox, N. & Roberts, C. (1999). GPs in cyberspace: The sociology of "virtual community." *Sociological Review, 47,* 643-671.

Heim, M. (1993). *The Metaphysics of virtual reality.* New York: Oxford University Press.

Hill, K. A. & Hughes, J. E. (1998). *Cyberpolitics: Citizen activism in the age of the Internet.* London: Rowman & Littlefield Publishers, Inc.

Kang, N. & Choi, J. H. (1999). Structural implications of the crossposting network of international news in cyberspace. *Communication Research, 26,* 454-481.

Ostrom, C. W. (1990). *Time series analysis: Regression techniques.* Newbury Park, CA: Sage.

Plant, S. (1997). *Zeros + Ones: Digital women + the new technoculture.* New York: Doubleday.

Postmes, T., Spears, R., & Lea, M. (1998). Breaching or building boundaries? SIDE-effects of computer-mediated communication. *Communication Research, 25,* 689-715.

Rice, R. E. & Love, G. (1987). Electronic emotion: Socioemotional content in a computer mediated communication network. *Communication Research, 14,* 85-108.

Taylor, T. L. (1999). Life in virtual worlds–plural existence, multimodalities, and other online research challenges. *American Behavioral Scientist, 43,* 436-449.

Wellman, B., Salaff, J., Dimitrova, D., Garton, L., Guila, M., & Haythorthwaite, C. (1996). Computer networks as social networks: Collaborative work, telework and virtual community. *Annual Review of Sociology, 22,* 213-238.

Wooley, B. (1992). *Virtual worlds: A journey in hype and hyperreality.* Oxford, UK: Blackwell.

Kermitt:
Conducting an Experiment on the Web

Paul Montgomery
David Ritchie

SUMMARY. A familiar and often difficult part of the research process is recruitment of subjects to participate in an experiment or survey. The World Wide Web offers potential access to a virtually unlimited pool of subjects: The trick is to administer an experiment in a smooth, apparently seamless manner. We describe a simple program for administering an experiment dependent on measuring response times over the Web. We discuss some of the problems we had to overcome, the trade-offs we faced, the reasons for the choices we made and the possible consequences of these choices. We then discuss possible applications to other research objectives. *[Article copies available for a fee from The Haworth Document Delivery Service: 1-800-HAWORTH. E-mail address: <getinfo@haworthpressinc.com> Website: <http://www.HaworthPress.com> © 2002 by The Haworth Press, Inc. All rights reserved.]*

KEYWORDS. Kermitt shell, automating research, bots

Paul Montgomery is a Communication Master's student at Portland State University, 1307 S.W. Broadway #402, Portland, OR 97201 (E-mail: kermitt@inetarena.com).

Dr. L. David Ritchie (PhD, Standford, 1987) is Associate Professor and Chair of the Department of Communication, Portland State University, P.O. Box 751, Portland, OR 97201 (E-mail: card@odin.pax.edu).

The authors would like to acknowledge Daniel Avila, whose insights have been helpful from the conceptualization of Kermitt to his final implementation.

[Haworth co-indexing entry note]: "Kermitt: Conducting an Experiment on the Web." Montgomery, Paul, and David Ritchie. Co-published simultaneously in *Journal of Technology in Human Services* (The Haworth Press, Inc.) Vol. 19, No. 2/3, 2002, pp. 135-149; and: *Using the Internet as a Research Tool for Social Work and Human Services* (ed: Goutham M. Menon) The Haworth Press, Inc., 2002, pp. 135-149. Single or multiple copies of this article are available for a fee from The Haworth Document Delivery Service [1-800-HAWORTH, 9:00 a.m. - 5:00 p.m. (EST). E-mail address: getinfo@haworthpressinc.com].

A thought to keep in mind: Milliseconds add up quickly.

INTRODUCTION

The World Wide Web, with potential access to millions of people, in principle provides an ideal way to recruit research subjects. A well-designed web site could draw hundreds of people each day, and it can draw people from a wide variety of demographic groups. The Web has already been used extensively for survey research; in this essay we describe a procedure for conducting an experiment online. We begin by describing the objectives and basic design of an experiment that we have conducted online, using a program called "Kermitt." We then describe the tools we used, the compromises that had to be made, and the reasoning behind the choices we made.

The purpose of our experiment was to test an hypothesis, first forwarded by Grice in 1968, about how people process metaphors. Reading and discrimination tasks are frequently used in this kind of cognitive research. The underlying assumptions are that thinking takes time, and more thinking takes more time. Hence, one can draw interesting inferences about how the mind actually processes different sorts of stimuli from the differences in processing time. Since our research question examined how metaphors are processed, we needed to compare the time it takes to process a metaphor with the time it takes to process a comparable literal. To measure processing time, we asked subjects to read a series of sentences, presented one at a time, and indicate whether the sentence makes sense or not. The primary technical requirements for this experiment were: to present the experimental task in an intuitive, easily comprehended way, to assign subjects randomly to experimental conditions, to obtain measures of actual response times sufficiently accurate to allow us to distinguish between actual differences and mere random noise, and to minimize the risk that some subjects would repeat the experiment two or more times, or otherwise compromise the assumptions of the experimental design. Obtaining a representative sample is probably unachievable, given that the method we used requires that subjects approach the site on their own volition. Fortunately, random assignment to experimental conditions is trivially easy, so the lack of a random sample is not fatal to the design. Moreover, compared with the standard technique of recruiting experimental subjects from a lower division college class, subjects recruited over the Web are likely to represent a more heterogeneous group. We were also concerned with subject recruitment and data recording, but these tasks proved relatively easy to solve, and will not be discussed here.

The problem of creating a time sensitive online experiment ought to be simple, and on one level it is. But the Devil lives in details: For example, to the extent that milliseconds add up quickly, and as our data are expressed in milliseconds, the Devil lives in making sure that neither the technical details of the experiment nor our subjects' reactions to our design choices artificially inflate response times. The test should not confuse or frustrate potential subjects, as both emotions engender affective responses that would introduce noise and complicate the interpretation of our findings. A related challenge facing experimenters is to increase sample size while minimizing the noise in the experimental data and keeping costs within budget–which, for a graduate student, means as low as possible.

KERMITT, AS SEEN FROM A SUBJECT'S POINT OF VIEW

The experiment begins when a subject points a browser to Kermitt's URL, and a page filled with contact information and an explanation of the experiment fills the screen. The on-screen explanation is deliberately a bit vague and verbose, in order to minimize the probability of return visits. The "next" button is at the bottom of the page, and does not appear on a subject's screen until the entire page has been scrolled. This page layout was meant to force potential subjects to read the explanation and introduction. Embedded in the "next" link is a JavaScript function call that serves to assign subjects, at random, into one of two testing conditions. A similar function could easily assign subjects into any number of test conditions, thus supporting an experimental design of any desired complexity.

The second page that a subject sees is filled with a brief, bolded and colored set of instructions: "Some passages will appear on the screen. If you think that the passage makes sense, strike the space bar to indicate a 'yes'. If you think that the passage does not make sense, strike any alphanumeric key to indicate a 'no'." Once subjects advance to the next page, they encounter a screen, split 80%/20%. Experimental stimuli are presented in the larger top frame; new passages are called into the top frame through a keyboard interface powered by a JavaScript that is located in the bottom frame. By striking alphanumeric keys, subjects cycle through the test. After subjects finish the test section of Kermitt they encounter a questionnaire, a couple of debriefing pages, and a comment box.

The first passages that the subjects see are all practice, and then the test apparently begins. In truth, the next five passages are also covert practice; we analyze only data from the final 15 stimuli. This helps to counter the "practice effect," minimizes the effect of self-consciousness induced by beginning the test and any early mistakes that might result from subjects' unfamiliarity with the procedures.

DESIGN CONSIDERATIONS

Commercial web sites attempt to be interesting, to work well with either of the dominant browsers, and to be easily navigable. In addition to these standard concerns, Kermitt needed to be accurate and operate uniformly across a range of unknown subjects. To summarize, our design was subject to the following constraints:

Be robust. Work well. And work well with either Netscape or Internet Explorer.

Be accurate. Measure actual response times, and minimize variance due to technical operations of the program as well as to non-task activities of the subjects.

Be intuitive. Either use or emulate normal web site conventions. Conform to subjects' expectations in a "transparent" way so the program does not call attention to itself and distract subjects. Minimize delays or equivocation due to task ambiguity.

Be quick. Make the program respond to the subjects in a "snappy" manner. Fast loading is a plus; fast response is a necessity.

Be slightly boring. We wanted the task to be sufficiently interesting that subjects would be motivated to complete it and recommend it to their friends, but not sufficiently interesting that they would be tempted to return to the site.

The value of being "robust" and "accurate" carry their worth prima facie and we will not attempt to explicate the obvious. The "quickness" and the "intuitive" injunctions do require some explanation: Quickly reacting to a user forestalls frustration. Having an intuitive site forestalls confusion. It would be best to avoid both frustration and confusion, but if faced with a Hobbesian choice, we would choose confusion over frustration. Our reasoning is that confused subjects will figure out the issue at hand, respond in an easily detectable "odd" manner, or simply leave the site. On the other hand, frustrated subjects may react in ways that are not easily predicted, and thus could add noise to the data. Attrition rate statistics can be used to detect whether subjects were more likely to become confused in one condition rather than another—a possible threat to validity.

In the next section, we detail some of the techniques we used to satisfy these constraints and the tradeoffs we made among them.

DESIGNING KERMITT

Goals: Accurately measure response times to a reading and discrimination task with a detection granularity of milliseconds.

Using the JavaScript DateObject to Capture Timing Data

Computers are busy creatures, with a variety of different operations in the air at any given time. They regulate these activities through an internal clock that resides in the "native machine" (each PC has one). This clock is not affected by the activity of the CPU. Upon receipt of a time request, the CPU takes a mere handful of microseconds to parse the request and respond.

At the start of each component of the test, Kermitt queries the clock for the time. When the subject next strikes a key, Kermitt gets the time again, and subtracts that time from the first time, with the remainder representing the time it took the subject to read and respond to the first passage.

It is also important that the call to the time method on the DateObject resides in a block of code as unencumbered as possible with nested loops and conditionals to be checked. The CPU's "attention" is divided by the number of operations it has running concurrently. These operations are executed one at a time. Either they queue up and are executed fully when their turn comes, or they are partially executed in a time shared manner, known as "multithreading." Both methods take time: The first forces a command to wait to be executed and the second executes commands in a piecemeal manner. Therefore, experiments that turn on accurately measuring milliseconds must have as few operations as possible when the time stamps are created.

For clarity's sake, we restate the above: There are two issues here. Getting the time, and knowing when to get the time. The actual getting of time takes nearly no time at all. It is merely a call to the system clock. But knowing when to get the time requires some minimal condition checking, and each condition that is checked is an operation that is cued up and performed when the CPU gets around to performing it. And even worse, there is no easy way of checking to see how long it takes any given command to be fully executed. Optimally, an outline of the time sensitive section of your program should look like this:

1: GET TIME
2: PRESENT STIMULUS
3: RESPONSE
4: GET TIME

And it should not look like this:

1: GET TIME
2: PRESENT STIMULUS
3: RESPONSE
4: CONDITION CHECKING
5: CONDITION CHECKING
6: CONDITION CHECKING
7: GET TIME

In writing your program, you might be tempted to place your condition checkers into the block of code that produces the time stamp. Why? Because the time stamp producing block of code will, most likely, be the nexus of your program. All relevant information will be sent to that block, and putting condition checkers there would serve to ease the programming of the site and also serve to make the total program cleaner. However, overall efficiency must be subordinated to the need for accuracy in measuring response times.

Using the Keyboard to Drive the User Interface
(Keyboard vs. Mouse)

Not to belabor the obvious, but we note again that milliseconds add up quickly. For our interface we used a keyboard to interface with the computer. Why? During the testing/building phase, our experiences showed that using the mouse to run the interface resulted in an added response time averaging nearly 200 ms., with an error variance ranging from +50 to +700 ms.

The behavior of the mouse device is unpredictable and we can think of many possible explanations for why this is so: Because the mouse is mobile across the screen it creates the possibility of users missing the target, or failing to click, but thinking they had. Sometimes, the mouse may be on or near the target, while other times the mouse is off in a corner, and so needs to be dragged over to the target. While most machines use a traditional mouse, some use a roller ball or touch pad. Finally, some mice stick frequently, some stick sporadically, and some never stick.

Randomize the Order of Presentation

Our test design called for the passages to be randomly presented. We accomplished this by filling an array up with a list of numbers, 0, 1, 2. The numbers that we used were an ID for a particular passage that was to be used in the test. Next, a pseudo-random number was generated between zero and the index of the last ID of array #1 and inserted into array #2. The ID at that index was then deleted from array #1. Array 1, when depleted, would then be overwritten by array #2, and the process repeated until the task of randomizing the array is completed. This provided us with a "random enough" array to assure that neither the test respondent nor we would know the order of the test statements before or during testing, while providing us with a key to determine after the fact which statement was being responded to during data analysis.

This shuffling technique is commonly used in computer-based card games. By way of trivia: A mere 32 iterations is all that is needed to shuffle a deck of 52 cards.

Attract Attention, but Avoid Test-Retakers

We wished to attract people to the site, and we were successful. In a month, with minimal effort on our part, we gathered 243 valid responses to the test. And we wanted all visitors to the site to be unique visitors, as test-retakers would introduce an element of experience as well as auto-correlation, and thus compromise the internal validity of the experiment.

One way to deal with test-retakers would be to set a cookie to identify machines from which the text had already been taken and toss any data gathered from machines that had already visited Kermitt. While this would create a loss in the total number of responses, it is an acceptable loss, and in our experience, recruiting subjects was not difficult.

However, cookie setting generates far more heat than light. Our Human Subjects Research Review Committee argued that the use of cookies would invalidate the anonymity of the test and raise several sticky ethical issues. Having had the issue decided against the use of cookies we were left with no active manner to detect who is visiting the site, so we decided to use a passive deterrent to raise the affective cost of returning to the site. We deliberately created an introductory section that featured boring prose, a turgid explanation and debriefing section, and the first practice passages were intentionally unmoving and devoid of light or poetry. Our hope was that the idea of the test would motivate people to spread Kermitt's URL amongst their friends and family, but the actual test itself would be so unengaging as to discourage people from revisiting the site.

Some Problems: Respecting All the Injunctions Equally Is Difficult

In principle, we tried to follow all of the above injunctions. However, compromises had to be made. The need to record the subject's response time accurately conflicted with our wish to be intuitive, as it interrupted the program flow of Kermitt. Our efforts to work equally well across platforms clashed with our efforts to make the site accurate, i.e., we lost some robustness, due to some "work arounds" in the HTML code that were needed in response to incompatibilities between the two most common browsers.

Using the Keyboard to Drive the Interface Complicates the Program Flow

Aside from being online, the "neatest" thing about Kermitt was that he uses the keyboard to drive the computer/user interface. His largest pitfall is that he uses the keyboard to drive the computer/user interface.

The vast majority of web sites are mouse controlled: The screaming weight of habit simply demands that our site, too, conform to the norms, on pain of confusing subjects. However, due to the reasons discussed in the foregoing, we felt that the common interface tool, the mouse, was simply too sloppy for our purposes. The predictable outcome was that some of our subjects did not know how to proceed. The issue was this: We did not use the mouse, but we needed a particular frame, containing the JavaScript, to be in focus (i.e., "activated"). A simple way to do that is to have the subject use the mouse once, click somewhere, anywhere in the target frame, and then use the keyboard to interface with Kermitt. We found that people balked. They wanted some more specific target to click on. But, had we used a button, a clickable area, or a link as a target, then that target would become focused, and not the frame with the JavaScript. The JavaScript would not be activated, and we could not collect the response time data.

During testing, we observed several people as they went through Kermitt, and found that about a fifth either failed to read the directions and/or just cannot figure out what they were supposed to do next. Some of those people quit; others read or reread the instructions and carried on.

Reduces the Compatibility of the Program

No test that uses a modified "snowball" method to gather subjects can get a truly random sample of the general population. This inherent problem was aggravated by our use of the JavaScript 1.2's keyboard listening device, which excluded older browsers. As there are still a large minority of computer users who do not have recent generation browsers, Kermitt was not as robust as our ideal program would have been.

People Want Quick Download Times, but Short Programs Lack the Power to Appear Simple

Kermitt is a collection of compromises. One of the most important considerations that went into his design was our wish to make him "lightweight." It would have been possible to write a program, perhaps in C, which would have been better than Kermitt in a host of ways. But it would not be practicable, as it would require subjects to download a C-based application, install it somewhere in their computer, then take the test. Somehow, it does not seem to us that many people would go through all those steps. Not only would few people go through such a heroic sequence of steps–those who would, are definitely not representative of the general population. Any approach we can think of that would minimize compromises at the level of technical design would raise similar issues.

MAKING KERMITT INTUITIVE

As mentioned, we attempted our best to make Kermitt snappy and "normal" in appearance. By way of example, to solve the frame focusing issue, all we needed the subject to do was to click the mouse anywhere in the correct frame and then strike any key. So we placed a simple comment in the target frame that read "click me," underscored it and set its font to blue, to make it look like a hyper-link. While it did not do anything, most people responded in the anticipated manner, clicked on it, then hit some key.

Correct Language Choice

Speed of response is the main requirement for being intuitive. People expect quick responses, and get frustrated if they are forced to wait for a computer to "catch up" with them. Tests with frustrated subjects measure affective reactions to stress as much as they measure whatever it is that the test/survey is designed to measure.

Choosing whether to use a client-side rather than a server-side-based program for your survey/experiment is of importance. Operating characteristics differ according to where the "heart" of a program resides, server-side or client-side. Server-side applications are the more traditional rubric. In those systems, an individual's computer is treated as a terminal, and it gets information transmitted to it and responds to commands from a program running on the main computer to which it is connected. In client-side programs, once a person makes a "hit" onto a web site a program is sent to that person's computer, where it then resides. These programs are called "applets" or "scripts." Each design has its own costs and benefits.

In principle, the primary weakness of client-side programs is that they cannot read from or write to disk. This is a built-in security precaution. The main advantage to client-side programs is that they are portable and serve to make programs interactive. This benefit brings in its train the single largest practical limitation to these kinds of programs: In practice, designers, with an eye towards making the load times of these portable programs reasonable, tend to make them small.

At first we built Kermitt as a distributed client/server networked program with a blend of Perl and Java. We used Java for the client-side timing mechanism and Perl to run the more complicated CGI scripts and to feed new passages into the subject's machine, over the network. As long as the client machine was on the same Local Area Network as the server machine, it was very quick.

But, once we moved off site, the response speed dropped precipitously. Technically, it worked, and it was as accurate as could be desired. The problem was that people did not take Kermitt seriously, as the latency times between when Kermitt would call the next passage and when it would get painted onto the screen, could be as long as half a second or more. This did not throw off the timing mechanism, as it only started once the screen was painted, but we received so many complaints that we decided to abandon the server-side rubric entirely.

Pre-Load All Stimuli

In an effort to speed the run time, we knew that we wanted to pre-load all the test stimuli, along with the HTML code. At first, we attempted to load each stimulus test passage into its own frame, set the frame size to zero, and call each test passage as needed. This would have been optimal, but we could not make it go. We are uncertain whether the problem was a code problem, a bug, or simply a bad idea.

To get around this issue, we made a single large HTML file and divided it up with internal reference tags and separated the different passages with enough blank lines to ensure that two would never be shown on the screen at the same time. The first time any part of the page was loaded, the entire document would be loaded. Our directions were at the very beginning of that document, so we knew each subject would necessarily see the directions before starting the test. While the subjects were occupied with reading the directions, the rest of the document was being loaded up. Thus we were able to hide our load times within the time required for subjects to read the directions.

A serious limitation with substantially long HTML documents that contain all the test passages is that anyone could view the source of the frame and see the text of the test. They would not know in what order the different passages would be presented, but they could read them. Furthermore, there is no way that we could know if they had viewed the source or not. Data from such subjects will probably be random "noise," but we cannot rule out the possibility of deliberate interference with the experiment. By leaving a sufficient number of blank lines between stimuli, the risk of subjects scrolling through the entire file is minimized–and careful inspection of the data will most likely suffice to detect such manipulation by subjects.

Reducing Download Times

For obvious reasons, we wanted quick download times. But we also wanted the site to run quickly. Compromises had to be made.

To help lessen the download times, we made the Kermitt as small as possible. While we did have a questionnaire and a debriefing section, it was loaded only after the subjects had already taken the actual test of Kermitt. A note: Of those who completed the timing section, 95% also completed the questionnaire section.

Another issue that requires a decision is whether to use a compiled language to code the test in, or a scripting one. Client-side compiled languages, though generally more powerful than client-side scripting languages, require a special environment known as a "virtual machine." This virtual machine turns its byte-code into a format runnable by the local machine. This incurs tremendous startup costs, as anyone who has visited a web page that uses Java or ActiveX can attest to. Despite the startup cost, once started, client-side compiled languages are more powerful and faster than client-side scripted languages. If we had chosen to use a compiled program, then we would have chosen to use Java, residing on the client-side. We would have loaded the entire Java applet and the stimuli into a JAR file (i.e., *J*ava *A*rchive *R*ecord file). For more complicated experiments, using a JAR is probably the best choice.

Client-side scripted languages generally use a lighter weight mechanism for execution known as an "interpreter." While the case can be made that all scripts must also be compiled into byte-code to be executed, the architecture of this process is different. Scripted languages almost exclusively bypass compile time data type checking and all but the most broad programming checks, leaving many errors such as misnamed variables and method calls to be found at run time. This decreases the startup cost at the expense of raising the runtime costs.

To defeat confusion, we restate some of the above: While it looks to the average user that the only issues here are "load time" and "run time," in truth, there are three: "load time," "start time" and "run time." It just so happens that slow start times have the same "look and feel" as slow load times. But 10K of data is 10K of data, no matter what language it is coded in. Therefore, to discuss the differences in load times between, say, Java (a compiled language) and JavaScript (an interpreted language), is to make a distinction without a difference. However, Java appears to load slowly, due to its compiler. In short: the perception is that client-side compiled languages take longer to load because of the startup cost.

For our needs, in an effort to lessen perceived load times while still running a quick enough program, we felt that the use of JavaScript represented an acceptable compromise. Also, we reduced actual load time by avoiding the use of images, while further reducing the perceived load time by hiding the HTML load time as described above.

INTERPRETING THE RESULTS: A WORD ABOUT STATISTICS

At first glance, the technical problems surrounding Kermitt's data collection method would seem to swamp whatever data that he gathered and would reduce it to just so much noise. For example: (1) We had no control over the setting in which our subjects participated. As one anonymous reviewer noted, while he was reading an earlier draft of this article, his cat climbed up on his keyboard to look at the screen. (2) We did not select our subjects, they selected us. (3) Some percent of our subjects surely had a background job in operation (e.g., perhaps a print job) while they were taking Kermitt's test. These would affect how accurately Kermitt could record their times. (4) Computers round tiny numbers, and worse than that, different computers round differently. And, (5) perhaps some of our test takers were repeat visitors.

Our first answer to these objections was to make all the responses relative to each subject. We normalized all response time data within subjects, then compared the within-subjects response across groups. We then compared each subject's observed time to his/her predicated time, for each passage, to determine the degree to which each subject's response differed from the predicated time. Our statistical analyses were performed over these numbers.

As a double check, we also analyzed the raw observed times. Both methods were in broad agreement, except that the raw numbers did display more statistical flutter.

Our second move to combat these pitfalls was to identify the responses that seemed to have been produced by non-complying subjects and/or distracted subjects, by looking for extreme outliers. We found that this was not a difficult task. Again, milliseconds add up quickly: And so those subjects who were not on task all the time were very conspicuous, and returned numbers several standard deviations away from their own response time norms. In response to one of our anonymous reviewers' questions; if a subject's cat walked across the keyboard at an inopportune time, that part of the data set would look very different from the rest of the data (although, alas, we have no way of knowing that an inquisitive cat was responsible for the aberration).

As to the fifth objection, we have no real defense, save that we did replicate our experiment using different subjects and obtained very similar results.

IMPLICATIONS FOR OTHER RESEARCH DESIGNS

The techniques described here would be easily amenable to more complicated designs. Our experiment was an example of a simple 2×2 test design, but much more complicated experimental designs would also be possible. Ours was a text-based experiment, but graphics or tones or some mix would also be possible.

In designing our experiment, we paid attention to our goals, experiment design, and our five test design considerations: Be robust, be accurate, be intuitive, be quick and be boring. However, different experiment goals would interplay with the design considerations differently.

For example, suppose that a researcher wished to conduct a "distraction-comprehension experiment" wherein the subjects' computers would sound a tone, or show some graphic, at selected times/places in some text. In order to do this in a seamless manner, the necessary code/modules would need to be preloaded into the subjects' browsers before the test could begin. As the file gets more complex, download times will increase: To keep the download time hidden from the subject might require a much longer set of instructions, or perhaps a distracting pre-test exercise of some sort.

Our code was relatively light-weight, so we needed only to pause our subjects for a few seconds before directing them to proceed. As we also wanted only unique visitors as subjects, in an attempt to discourage multiple visits, we elected to slow our subjects down with a deliberately vague and boring set of directions. As noted, if a program would need longer load times to pre-load itself correctly, then the design should display an interesting front page, so that potential subjects would loiter there for awhile, before moving into the actual experiment.

Using this technique could also benefit survey researchers by facilitating the measurement of response times. For example, it would allow the researcher to identify subjects who took the survey lightly, by detecting those who took it too quickly. At a more sophisticated level, measuring response times might allow a researcher to identify questionnaire items that pose difficulties for subjects. It might even be possible to identify subjects who spend time "second-guessing" certain questions, by looking at overall patterns of response times within subjects. Also, it would be possible to detect if and when subjects had changed their answers to a survey.

On Likert-type scales, a researcher could determine whether extreme responses seem to take more or less time than middle-of-the-road responses. On open-ended questionnaires, measuring response-latency would provide a good way to ascertain whether responses were "off-the-top-of-the-head" or if they were first carefully considered.

One anonymous reviewer suggested that something like this technique might be useful in an agency intranet "where response time is monitored to try to get at the accuracy of data entry into an intranet-based MIS. For example, if responses to a risk assessment form were completed too quickly, it might indicate that the worker was not thinking about the case, but just responding as quickly as possible. If this were occurring often, the worker and the supervisor might be notified that central administration is concerned because response time is too fast (or too slow)." To carry the reviewer's suggestion a bit further, the data gathered in this manner could be used to identify unexpectedly difficult or poorly worded sections of questionnaires or forms.

It has become commonplace to use the power of the Web as a tool for interactive and partially interactive communication with a potentially unlimited number of people. Since partially interactive communication with a large number of people is a primary objective of researchers, the Web seems to offer a natural tool for research. The problem is how to overcome some of its current technical limitations so as to achieve a required degree of methodological rigor.

We have described the technical details of an online self-administered experiment, called "Kermitt," and the design considerations that went into him. We have described the compromises that had to be made, the reasoning behind our choices, and the effects of our choices on the validity of the experiment. Finally, we suggested some possible applications of a similar program to other research situations. In general, Kermitt represents a type of Web-based program that is relatively robust, easy to build and install, easy for subjects to use, and is serviceable for a wide variety of research objectives. We used Kermitt to measure response times as a basis for drawing inferences about how people process metaphors, but a similar program could be adapted to serve many other familiar research objectives.

Index